FROZEN BRITAIN

GAVIN COOKE

FROZEN BRITAIN

HOW THE BIG FREEZE OF 2010 IS THE BEGINNING OF BRITAIN'S NEW MINI ICE AGE

JOHN BLAKE

Published by John Blake Publishing Ltd,
3 Bramber Court, 2 Bramber Road,
London W14 9PB, England

www.johnblakepublishing.co.uk

First published in paperback in 2010

ISBN: 978 184454 989 4

British Library Cataloguing-in-Publication Data:

A catalogue record for this book is available from the British Library.

Design by www.envydesign.co.uk

Printed in Great Britain by CPI Bookmarque, Croydon CRO 4TD

1 3 5 7 9 10 8 6 4 2

Papers used by John Blake Publishing are natural, recyclable products made
from wood grown in sustainable forests. The manufacturing processes
conform to the environmental regulations of the country of origin.

CONTENTS

INTRODUCTION
30 FREEZING WINTERS

What happened to the weather this winter? It started to get really cold just before Christmas, then there were ten extreme weather warnings from the Met Office on New Year's Day. In the week that followed, heavy snow blanketed northern England and Scotland. Wasn't all this supposed to be a thing of the past now that global warming was a settled science?

It turned out to be a lot worse than anyone expected. Despite most New Year celebrations passing off without too much inconvenience, revellers celebrating the end of 'the noughties' were about to be served up the kind of whiteout not seen in Britain for nearly 30 years. The freezing weather that blew over Britain after Christmas came despite the Met Office's long-range forecast, published in October, of a mild winter. That followed its earlier prediction of a 'barbecue summer', a summer which actually saw the wettest July recorded for almost 100 years.

By New Year's Eve, those who had no other alternative but to drive in order to visit relatives or stock up on supplies in parts of Northumberland, Cumbria and the Scottish Highlands were warned not to travel unless absolutely necessary.

However, the freezing temperatures were good news for the skiers. One Cairngorm ski centre in the eastern highlands of Scotland said it had its best Christmas holiday season in 14 years with more than 8,000 skiers and snowboarders using its runs, nearly a thousand of them on New Year's Day.

Across the northern hemisphere, snow was also falling heavily, and it turned out to be the second snowiest December since records began. On Friday, 8 January 2010, it was widely reported in the press that parts of Britain were as cold as the South Pole and that this was the coldest spell of weather seen in almost 30 years. In the coldest night for 14 years, the temperature dropped to -22°C (-7.6°F) in the Scottish Highlands, with bitterly cold temperatures reported almost everywhere else in the UK.

There were also tragedies. On 9 January 2010, *BBC News* reported that two brothers had died after falling through the ice over a frozen lake in Leicestershire. Police also confirmed that 24 other people in Britain had died in weather-related incidents in the first nine days of the New Year. As the week dragged on and waves of snow cascaded across the country, Perth, in central Scotland, had its fleet of gritters grounded because of the -10°C (14°F) cold, leaving roads untreated.

Perth and Kinross Council said their gritters weren't able even to leave the depot because the extreme weather had led to difficulties in refuelling their vehicles.

The freeze left roads and pavements covered in ice, and drivers were warned not to take their cars out without an emergency blanket, shovel and thermos. Those venturing out on foot found that walking anywhere was both time-consuming and dangerous.

The extreme weather featured in that day's cabinet meeting, with the Transport Secretary Lord Adonis telling his colleagues that so much grit was being used up that council gritters had stopped treating motorway hard shoulders in an effort to save reserves. Such was the demand that the government set up what it termed 'Salt Cell', an emergency body responsible for deciding how salt stocks were allocated.

Environment Secretary Hilary Benn admitted that supplies of natural gas were low but dismissed concerns about shortages, as the National Grid had been obliged to force many large UK firms to turn off their gas supplies after a record demand from UK households.

Overnight, temperatures in Manchester fell to -15°C (5°F), with Glasgow reaching -8°C (18°F), Cardiff -5°C (23°F) and London hovering just below zero (32°F).

The lowest temperature in the Scottish Highlands that night did indeed come close to the -22.9°C (-9.2°F) being experienced at the South Pole, but didn't break Braemar's 10 January 1982 record of the lowest temperature ever recorded in Britain, -27.2°C (-16.9°F).

In most winters, and certainly those we've seen over the last 30 years or so, our winds have come from the south-west. Normally, warm air travelling over a relatively warm Atlantic Ocean means we get mild winters here in Britain. Not this year, though, because from the end of December 2009 mild Atlantic air was blocked from travelling along its usual route by a heavy, stationary mass of cold air that flowed down from the Arctic and the cold winter landmasses of Eastern Europe and Siberia.

Whenever cold, dry air moves away from the frozen poles, it eventually meets up with warmer, wetter air moving away from the warm equator. When warm, moist air meets cold air, condensation occurs and precipitation or rain is the result. If the temperature is below zero, this precipitation falls as snow. This winter an atmospheric pattern developed over the

Arctic Circle that flushed cold air away from the North Pole towards the mid-latitudes, where we in Britain are located. This pattern, known as high-latitude blocking, is essentially a large area of high pressure (or anticyclone). It pushed cold air downwards and as that air got nearer the surface of the Earth it was forced outwards, sending the cold air toward us. The ensuing freeze was the product of an Arctic Oscillation (AO), a weather pattern that sees the development of these blocking areas of high pressure in northern latitudes that drive polar winds much further to the south than they should normally be. This blocking pattern was the strongest on record for any December and came in two separate parts.

The first, over Greenland, blocked the usual warmer, westerly winds from reaching Europe across the Atlantic by steering the high-altitude Jet Stream far to the south of Britain, leaving us and north-western Europe exposed to winds from Russia, Scandinavia and the Arctic Ocean. Because of this, our Jet Stream, the fast warm wind that circles the globe from west to east, pushing wet but mild Atlantic weather systems across Britain during the winter months, did not end up over the English Channel where it should be. Instead, it was shunted across and down to the Strait of Gibraltar towards the Mediterranean. The second anti-cyclone was Siberian in origin and settled cold air on large areas of the USA as well as Western Europe and across to China.

In a nutshell, the weather that north-western Europe usually gets from the Jet Stream was diverted south towards Spain and the Mediterranean, hundreds of miles south of its normal position for this time of year. This allowed Crete to post a record January high of 40°C (104°F). As a result, we in Britain froze.

The Met Office assured us that all was as it should be, and in line with the larger picture of continuous global warming, but other experts are not so sure.

There is now a strong body of scientific opinion that says Britain and northern Europe are headed for a lengthy period of colder weather in the coming century before the effects of man-made global warming kicks in.

In 2002, the National Academy of Sciences, the board of academics established to advise the US government on scientific matters, compiled a report called 'Abrupt Climate Change: Inevitable Surprises'.

The 244-page report, which contains over 500 references, was written by a team of 59 of the top researchers on climate, and represented the most authoritative source of information about abrupt climate change available. What they agreed on was that global warming is responsible for the melting of the Greenland ice sheet and polar sea ice, which increases the amount of fresh water flowing into deep-water formation areas around Greenland. What they needed to know was what effect this would have on the weather.

Our satellites are pretty good at measuring overall ocean temperatures from space, and CO_2 measurements are being taken daily from around the globe. So far, we know from satellite data that CO_2 increases appear about nine months after an upswing in ocean temperatures, but what does it all mean for Joe Public?

Here was the big shock contained in the report, a predicted 20-feet sea-level rise within decades. This tended to focus the minds of strategic planners in the developed world.

After the report and its alarming conclusions, scientific advisers to our own government became concerned about the prospect of a sudden shutdown of the Meridional Overturning Circulation (MOC), a global network of density-driven ocean currents, also referred to as the thermohaline circulation (THC), which is potentially catastrophic for Britain. The MOC transports a tremendous amount of heat northwards, keeping the North Atlantic and much of Europe up to 5°C (41°F) warmer in the winter than *No!* our northerly latitude deserves.

A sudden shutdown of this current would have a

time-factored ripple effect throughout the ocean-atmosphere system, with huge changes in temperature. The most affected areas would be Britain, northern Europe and the eastern United States of America.

Look at a globe or a map of the world. Running from east to west are lines known as lines of latitude, which are a measure of how far north or south a land mass lies from the equator.

The equator runs right through the middle of the world at 0 degrees. Trace the line of the equator with your forefinger and you will see it runs through countries like Brazil, Colombia and Kenya. These are hot countries, because the equator gets the most heat from the sun, directly above, throughout the year. As you move further north, it gets colder because not only are you getting closer to the Arctic, where all the ice is, but also the sun's rays hit the earth at a greater angle and so heat the areas of land they strike less intensely.

At 90°N of the equator is the North Pole. At 66.5°N of the equator is the Arctic Circle, frozen solid for most of the year. Just below this, at 54°N lies Britain, not that far away from the Arctic. Place your forefinger on this 54°N line of latitude and trace it west and you will end up at Labrador on the north-east coast of Canada, frozen all winter. Typical January daytime temperatures are -15°C (5°F). Summers there are also chilly because of the cold

Labrador current. The Labrador Sea is filled with floating ice and icebergs for up to eight months of the year and summer brings widespread fog driven by moist easterly winds. In July, the temperature in Labrador may, if you're lucky, climb to a not so balmy 8°C (46.4°F) along the coast. The home of the Eskimos, it rarely warms up enough to make it worthwhile for them to take off their fur-lined boots.

There but for the grace of God we go, because, joined as we are on the same latitude as Labrador and central Siberia, we should have the same weather... but we don't because of one miraculous anomaly, the moderating influence of the Gulf Stream.

It's only in the last ten years or so, with the aid of advanced computer modelling, that scientists have nailed down the connection between the movements of the Gulf Stream, also known as the Great Conveyor Belt, and the relatively warm climate of Western Europe (*fig 1*). They found that the Gulf Stream brought warm water north from the tropics, around the Gulf of Mexico then on up to Latitude 40°N, about where Portugal is, where the current splits in two. Half goes south in a current known as the subtropical gyre while the other half, the North Atlantic Drift, continues on towards Britain where its heat helps warm us up by between 5°C (41°F) and 10°C (50°F) during the winter.

No!

No!

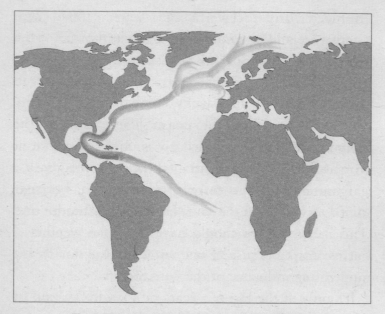

Fig 1: The flow of the gulf stream in the Atlantic.

That's 27,000 times as much as all the heat produced from all the power stations in Britain. Without this Great Conveyor Belt, we would be in the same boat, climatologically, as the Eskimos. Only worse, because our ability to carry all but a fraction of our current population of almost 62 million would be wiped out. You can't grow food under a sheet of ice.

Scientists have lately come to appreciate what a marvel of thermodynamics the Gulf Stream really is, driven by differences in temperature and salinity. Simply put, salty water is heavier/denser than freshwater and the warm salty water of the Great Conveyor Belt gets colder as it moves north until it reaches a point just off the southern tip of Greenland where the heat keeping it near the surface gets obliterated by the cold winds of North America. It's at this point that this huge mass, a falling column of cold salty water some ten miles across, drops like a stone to the bottom of the Atlantic where it becomes a gargantuan undersea torrent, many times larger than all the rivers in the above-ground world combined. This dense feature then moves off to begin another cycle of its journey and by doing so draws in a strong surface current of warm salty water to replace it.

This fresh supply of warm salty water comes up through the South Atlantic past the Gulf of Mexico and warms the chilly shores of Britain all winter. This is the Gulf Stream in action, a continuous supply of water energy, a huge liquid mass running to the Pacific then back to the Atlantic in a loop that takes 1,000 years to complete. Because this Great Ocean Conveyor Belt is driven by differences in ocean water density, the danger is that if it is diluted somehow it will slow, and we won't get that extra heat in winter.

Unfortunately, this is already happening. Scientists have shown that global warming has melted huge quantities of glacial fresh water which has then flushed its way into the Atlantic in crucial areas on either side of Greenland where the Gulf Stream waters cool and sink. This has lessened the ocean's level of salinity – and hence its density – enough so that the waters are no longer sinking as fast and the Gulf Stream current has started to slow.

One theory says our current run of very mild winters, up to 2008/09 has been due to global warming powering up Atlantic weather systems coming from the west. With more energy, these systems can travel further east and hence prevent the big Siberian high-pressure zones moving our way and dominating our weather. Once this colder, denser air from Russia is in place, it stays put, giving us heavy snowfall, frosts and bitter east winds for weeks at a time.

Computer models simulating ocean-atmosphere climate dynamics indicate that our North Atlantic region would cool 3°C (37.4°F) to 5°C (41°F) if conveyor circulation were totally disrupted. This might not sound much but it would result in winters twice as cold as the worst winters on record here or in the eastern United States in the past century. In addition, previous conveyor shutdowns have been linked with widespread droughts throughout the globe.

As Britain froze last winter, the Met Office repeated its conventional wisdom that this was of no long-term significance. This was nothing unusual: don't worry, the climate is still warming.

The Met Office expects that the UK's normally mild and wet winters will become increasingly warmer and wetter as a result of climate change, with this effect expected to be most pronounced towards the latter part of this century. This was the conclusion drawn by the Intergovernmental Panel on Climate Change (IPCC), the world's authority on climate-change issues. It was established in 1988 under the auspices of the United Nations (UN) Environment Programme and the World Meteorological Organization with the stated aim of assessing 'the scientific, technical and socio-economic information relevant for the understanding of the risk of human-induced climate change', and it is composed of representatives appointed by governments and policy-making organisations

The IPCC does not carry out any new research nor does it monitor climate-related data. Its main function is to base its assessments of how the climate is changing on published and peer-reviewed scientific technical literature. The IPCC has been examining the likelihood of man-made global warming since it was formed, and such is its authority that when it speaks of climate change the world takes notice, and the IPCC says that man-made CO_2 is responsible for global warming. Over time, the IPCC has become the most important adviser to governments on climate-related issues that now dominate the international political agenda. The way it works is that once the IPCC scientists have drafted their reports they are circulated to the government officials of all the countries involved. These scientists and officials come together to agree, line by line, the wording of each summary report for policymakers. The consensus is all, and rarely, if ever, do any of its members break ranks and disagree with any of the conclusions.

Among the most prominent of these member scientists is Professor Mojib Latif, who leads a research team at the renowned Leibniz Institute at Germany's Kiel University. He is famous for having developed new methods for measuring ocean temperatures 3,000 feet beneath the surface, where the cooling and warming cycles start.

Surprisingly, given that Latif is part of the IPCC consensus that says man-made global warming is a settled science, he and his colleagues have now predicted a new cooling trend. Latif's research has focused on the influence of cyclical changes to ocean currents and temperatures in the Atlantic which he describes as the North American Oscillation and this in turn relates to much longer-term shifts, known as the Pacific and Atlantic 'multi-decadal oscillations' (MDOs).

It was at the beginning of the 20th century that climatologists began to understand better the changes in sea-level pressures that take place between Iceland

and the Azores and the way these differences influence the strength of the westerly winds that blow in our direction. This difference was called the North Atlantic Oscillation (NAO). Scientists said that when the pressure difference between these two areas is large the NAO is in a positive phase. This results in a large amount of warm moist air coming off the Atlantic Ocean and then moving on to northern Europe. However, when these air-pressure systems are weak over Iceland and the Azores, the NAO moves into a negative phase and there are a lot fewer storms reaching northern Europe, and those that do are much weaker. This has the effect of cooling the region significantly. For Europe, the most important factor at work here is the temperature of the water right in the middle of the North Atlantic, which last winter was several degrees below its seasonal average. A negative NAO seems to have been the dominant system between 1650 and 1710 when, as we shall see later, a Little Ice Age prevailed over Europe, and there were very low numbers of sunspots (as there are now), a period known as the Maunder minimum. At the same time, the Gulf Stream was slowing down, transporting about 10 per cent less warm water north, and as less heat was coming up from the tropics so it began to get colder and colder. The combination of these events led to a mini ice age in Britain and the same sequence of events is leading to the cooling of the North Atlantic region again now. We are on the verge of another small ice age. In a paper published in 2008, Professor Latif warned, 'A significant share of the warming we saw from 1980 to 2000 and at earlier periods in the 20th Century was due to these cycles – perhaps as much as 50 per cent.' (1)

When he factored these fluctuations into his global climate model, he found that the results contradicted the consensus view of global temperatures, as set out in the IPCC's reports. These cycles, he said, 'have now gone into reverse, so winters like this one will become much more likely. Summers will also probably be cooler, and all this may well last two decades or longer. The extreme retreats that we have seen in glaciers and sea ice will come to a halt. For the time being, global warming has paused, and there may well be some cooling.' (2)

Latif concluded that our planet had, in fact, not warmed for nearly a decade and that it was likely that we were about to enter 'one or even two decades during which temperatures cool'.

Although Latif still thinks a warming trend will resume in the longer term, he also asserts that all the empirical evidence uncovered points to cooling, a blip or pause in this longer warming trend. This revelation of a possible 20 or 30-year cooling phase was repeated at an IPCC conference in Geneva in September 2009.

There were few sunspots visible during the Little Ice Age, and this is the other significant variable leading us towards colder temperatures. From July to August 2009, there were a nearly unprecedented 51 consecutive days without a sunspot, one day short of the record. As of 15 September 2009, solar cycle 23, with 717 spotless days since 2004, was the third longest on record. This is also important because, as we shall see, it's not global warming we have to worry about over the next 30 years, but a semi-permanent return of arctic conditions.

CHAPTER ONE

THE FREEZER BEFORE
THE FRYING PAN

Britain abolished slavery in the 19th century but replaced the work done by a different kind of slave in the 20th, one derived from the cheap and seemingly limitless resource of fossil fuels. Oil was a slave that could work the land without the need of rest or wages and produce huge amounts of food for next to nothing. Throughout the last century right up to the present day, fertilisers and nitrates, made by oil-based products, could grow enough food to effortlessly feed more than 6 billion people.

Oil is basically dead organic material that has accumulated on the bottom of oceans, riverbeds or swamps over hundreds of thousands of years mixing in with mud and sand. Over aeons, more and more of this sediment piles on top, creating heat and pressure which transforms the organic layer into a dark substance known as kerogen. Over time, and depending on how liquid or gaseous the kerogen is, it will turn into either oil or natural gas.

In 1956, MK Hubbert became the best-known geophysicist in the world after he presented a paper to assembled executives of the American oil industry in San Antonio, Texas, in which he showed conclusively that America's conventional crude-oil production would peak in 1970 and then start to decline. His prediction was absolutely accurate but ignored by those who were to see the benefits of fossil-fuel revenues create a new and permissive society that was to last until the first oil shock of 1973.

In 1967, the Beatles sang 'All You Need Is Love' to a worldwide audience of more than a billion, and the western world was united in a summer of love as the gilded youth of middle-class families looked forward to a long and easy life etched with adventure and possibilities.

Future generations will see that sunny June day as the highest peak of collective optimism ever experienced by the world as it was. Following that brief shining moment comes a long decline that will culminate in the collapse of our oil-based industrial civilisation, a mere 70 years later.

Hubbert would not have been at all surprised that the energy shortages that followed the savage winters of the 21st century in Britain then became a series of economic recessions, the first of which took place in 2008 following a sustained period of economic growth. Massive amounts of taxpayers' money pumped into the coffers of western banks temporarily alleviated the situation but only until the next recession came hard on its heels a few years later. This may be the way future historians record what happened.

The real process of decline began in the winter of 2009. The 12 warmest years in meteorological history had all been recorded since 1990 accompanied by a succession of mild winters but the winter of 2009/10 was the coldest in almost 30 years. High pressure and cold air from Siberia dominated the weather from December onwards, bringing snow and yet more snow. Britain, as usual, was caught unprepared. Roads were closed and council gritters ran out of grit. For most meteorologists, this was nothing out of the ordinary. After all, it was surely the preceding run of mild winters that deserved comment, not one that conformed to the norm before 1990.

The winter of 2012/13 came as a shock to the system. The sun shone throughout the summer of 2012 as Britons basked in the heat and revelled in the party atmosphere accompanying the Olympic Games.

Winter came early that year, dominated by an

intensely cold wind that blew in from the frozen steppes of Siberia. Freezing fog closed most of Britain's airports in November and London recorded a 5 November midday temperature of -12°C (10.4°F). A brief respite from the Arctic winds allowed those who were spending Christmas in sunnier climes a window to escape the icy blast. They were the lucky ones.

On 21 December, Atlantic weather systems and the rain associated with them pushed into the UK from the south-west. The result was heavy snowfall that blanketed most of the country, giving Britain its first real white Christmas Day for many years.

To begin with, the party atmosphere, a remnant of the summer games still strong in the collective memory, spilled over into the general population who celebrated the kind of Christmas only Charles Dickens could have imagined. No school, no work and a winter wonderland of snow cloaking the country to play in. Rivers became skating rinks as they froze over and hillsides a paradise for skiers and sledging enthusiasts. The novelty soon wore off, though. Significant amounts of snow continued to fall on and off for the next six weeks. Drifts of more than 25 feet were reported in Scotland in January as the relentless whiteout brought transport in Britain to a standstill.

FROZEN BRITAIN

All shipping has to be suspended as gales driving fierce snow storms batter the coastal ports. With points frozen solid, the train timetables are scrapped. Power lines covered in ice collapse and the resulting power cuts leave thousands of homes temporarily dependent on candlelight in the depths of winter. Those still with power watch the news to see reports of frozen bodies being dug out of abandoned cars, snow drifts and isolated farmhouses. Abandoned Lorries clog the motorways, stuck fast in compacted snow even the collective efforts of snowploughs, bulldozers and mechanical diggers fail to shift.

The sun didn't shine at all in February and by the end of the month those unfortunate enough to live in the country had all but run out of food. Emergency supplies of milk and bread are dropped by helicopter to hospitals and old folks' homes. Frozen or burst pipes mean little or no fresh water to drink. If there is no standpipe in the immediate vicinity, people must boil frozen snow.

The death toll mounts steadily from dozens to hundreds as, by early March, the iron grip of winter shows no sign of relaxing its grasp on beleaguered Britain. By now industry has virtually ground to a halt. With no trains, buses or cars running, most of the workforce decides to sit it out at home and absenteeism clocks in at over 50 per cent. Hospitals struggle to cope with the victims of a new wave of influenza sweeping the nation as well as those suffering from exposure, frostbite and broken bones. All cross-border roads into Scotland are cut off by huge snowdrifts and the locals are forced to cut down trees or scavenge for wood to burn on open fires.

The last heavy falls of snow come at the end of April stopping all traffic to the coast from London. Finally, in early May warm winds bring a thaw to ice-bound Britain, and daytime temperatures of 13°C (55.4°F).

The nation heaves a collective sigh of relief, but the worst isn't over yet. Low pressure brings torrential rain which is unable to penetrate the still frozen subsoil and so runs off in torrents. The river Severn and Wye burst their banks and flood Herefordshire and Gloucestershire. Vast areas of southern Britain including Oxford, the Fenlands and all of Southern Ireland are completely under water. Mud landslides cause more fatalities and the cost of cleaning it all up is estimated at tens of billions.

This is money the Treasury doesn't have after borrowing billions to pay for an economic stimulus following the credit crunch of 2009. Britain is effectively broke and, as in 1976, must go to the International Monetary Fund (IMF) for a crisis loan.

The following six years see traditional weather patterns temporarily re-emerging only to be disrupted again. There is a run of six summers without any significant periods of sun, characterised by heavy winds, increased rainfall and a year-on-year decrease in average temperatures of 5°F. There is significantly less rainfall over Europe as a whole, down by 30 per cent, leading to crop failure and food-price inflation.

Opinion among weather forecasters and climatologists is divided. Some believe that this is just another meteorological blip and that this run of cool, wet weather in the UK will soon end. Those who predict a new ice age or global drought are contradicted by the government's own experts. The public are told there is nothing to worry about but many suspect that they are not being told the whole truth.

In fact, the government is in possession of a report from a team of oceanographers based at a leading university detailing conclusive evidence of the slowing of the THC system and the near certainty that Britain is about to enter a mini ice age that could last anything up to 50 years, or until man-made global warming has some moderating effect.

This is the lull before the storm and the general public going about their daily business commonly remark on the strange weather, so many high winds and fierce storms, where have our English summers gone, how much colder it is in spring.

October 2019 brings the second great winter of the 21st century with a blocking anticyclone from the East reducing temperatures to below -20°C on ten successive nights in London. Significant amounts of snow fall throughout that month and Scotland is again cut off from the rest of the country, swamped under 25 feet snowdrifts. By December, there is no water supply north of the border as all feeder streams leading to its reservoirs have become ice-bound.

South of the border, there is significant snowfall over Christmas and the New Year. Shops, restaurants and cafes are closed. No trains or buses are running. Lorries lie abandoned as diesel freezes in their engines. The Thames freezes as far as Windsor and the sea is solid ice 100 metres out from Dover. The harbour there is like a skating rink and the army have to use amphibious vehicles to get supplies to hospitals on the south coast. A bad situation is made worse by strike action from power and oil-refinery workers, who come out in protest over the use of foreign labour, and then by hospital staff who strike after exhausted workers demand greater overtime payments.

The coalition government invokes the Emergency Powers Act to allow the army to take over the running of oil refineries but fails to quell the outcry in the NHS, and the crisis rumbles on.

Hundreds of pensioners die of the extreme cold,

many found frozen indoors, too frightened to put on their central heating because of escalating utility bills. Most are killed by severe exposure, reports social services. Some voluntary workers on mercy missions report icicles hanging from the inside of their homes. The power companies increase their tariffs by over 200 per cent in January and that month a foot of snow falls in under an hour, the fastest blizzard ever known. By the end of February, the country has endured 60 consecutive days with temperatures below zero. The sea freezes around all Britain's coastal waters, the River Tyne to a depth of 16 inches. Even the salt used to clear the roads freezes.

Food shortages are now severe almost everywhere. Farmers attempt to dig up potatoes, turnips and parsnips using picks, shovels and even pneumatic drills. The rock-hard topsoil means they are unable to plough fields or plant crops. There will be no harvest in 2020. The government bans the export of food and fuel and requests aid from the EU. Potatoes and bread appear on the ration for the first time since 1947, and bartering for food becomes widespread.

From above, Britain appears as a solid sheet of ice, immobile and stricken. British Summer Time begins in March with another 10 inches of snow falling within an hour. In the far north of Scotland, people leave their houses from their bedroom windows and walk rooftop to rooftop on compacted snow: drifts reach the top of telegraph poles. Food riots break out in most of Britain's major cities and troops are called out to quell disorder. Food rationing is disrupted by armed gangs with automatic weapons that rob and murder at will in the absence of any significant police or army presence on the streets. Fur boots and coats, mountain gear and ski equipment are the thieves' most prized targets. Stores selling winter or arctic gear are able to charge what they like. Sledges become the normal mode of transport for many Britons; those who can't buy them make them from planks of wood stripped from council property.

By early May, most of the north of Britain is still snowbound. A thaw in the south raises temperatures to above 10°C (50°F) for the first time in nine months. Some semblance of summer at last, but with it comes severe flooding and Londoners are left without any clean drinking water after the pumping station at Lea Bridge is submerged. Britain has effectively run out of food: no butter, milk or fish. Even priority drops of dairy to hospitals fail to arrive and it is clear that the UK can no longer carry a population close to 70 million. Panic sets in when a report detailing the partial shutdown of the Atlantic Conveyor system is leaked. Thousands take to the streets demanding food and fuel. Dustbins full of uncollected refuse are overrun by rats. Burst water pipes go unrepaired and cases of dysentery are documented by several hospital trusts.

In desperation, the government extends British Summer Time to November but before it expires the snow comes back again, in October. Most large insurance companies declare themselves bankrupt after claims go above and beyond any prospect of ever being met.

In London, there is the rumour of a cholera outbreak. Television news describes how animals have been killed for food and bread and vegetables are sold on the black market. The unrest escalates but protestors are driven off the streets by blizzards as heavy snow continues to fall from December to February. Prison riots break out everywhere as inmates starve; a woman carrying a loaf of bread is attacked and injured by starving pigeons. Farmers report crows attacking and killing sheep, pecking out their eyes before devouring their carcases. Rats, in huge numbers, begin to openly invade homes, attacking householders when confronted. There are even reports of babies being attacked in their prams by the starving rodents. Food for livestock runs out completely and sheep are reported to be eating the bark off trees before starving to death.

The Conservative government collapses, unable to

secure a mandate, and an election in June leads to its forming a coalition government with the United Britain Party, who come to power with the slogan 'British Jobs for British Workers' and an authoritarian manifesto aimed at reducing the surplus population by means of forced deportation of illegal immigrants and non-European citizens.

A desperate effort from governments around the globe tries to kick-start traditional economic growth, but, without the necessary quantities of cheap oil on tap, only succeeds in producing rampant inflation followed by deflation followed by inflation until a great depression settles on the whole system choking off world trade.

Basic greed from an unreformed banking system and the false optimism of economists who believed that as oil became scarcer the market would provide a solution to the energy crisis has led to disaster. There will be no back to business as usual: even the bankers' collective assumption that oil prices would continue to rise was proven to be false. Germany and France have also been devastated by the cold and an appeal is made to the USA for urgent aid. Those who sense the hopelessness of the situation now load their cars with whatever possessions they think can be sold on at their final destination. Homes in the UK are abandoned, their property value now close to zero.

The majority head for Spain or Italy, some for Tunisia or Morocco, anywhere warmer. However, not only the British are on the move. Scandinavia has been totally devastated by the freak weather and more than 30 per cent of its population are also heading south as are those able to get out of Ireland and Iceland.

Iceland has suffered 18 months of continuous frosts and deep-lying snow and has watched helplessly as 10 per cent of its population have perished in the cold. With TV and radio broadcasts severely censored and power rationing still in place, most of the millions on the move are not aware that they will need to move a lot further south than they think to escape the freeze. In July, roads out of London clear just long enough to permit the start of a mass exodus of people wanting to flee the country, and 75,000 cars an hour leave London for the coast. France, itself battered by the intense cold, protests, but can do nothing to prevent the free movement of EU citizens allowed under the Lisbon Treaty. Like 1940 in reverse, remarks one French commentator on the flood of refugees coming their way. Temperatures in Bavaria have dropped below -20°C, most of Spain is shivering at just above zero and there is snow in Tunisia.

To the dismay of all, the winter of 2020 follows the same pattern as the winter of 2019.

Each year after 2020 produces a winter more

savage than the last and the price of oil and natural gas rocket. Crude-oil prices breach $200 a barrel but it is already too late to make the investments needed in the industrial infrastructure to allow renewable energy to seamlessly flow its way to the grid. Less cheap energy means global manufacturing and transportation slow to a trickle. Slowly at first, then at a gathering pace, worldwide industrial production grinds to a halt and then flatlines, along with the price of oil. There is nothing being made, nothing to buy and no money to buy it with. The irony for Western economies is that they had outsourced their precious manufacturing infrastructure overseas to take advantage of cheap foreign labour. Those machine-made miracles of mass production that churned out everything from razor blades to cargo pants were now marooned in the sweatshops of India or China. America and Britain found that, with no money left, and more significantly, no more cheap energy that could be used to re-establish an indigenous manufacturing base, their ability to mass-produce had been lost for good.

Gradually the rot set in, hordes of desperate and frightened people queued day and night outside the few shops left with anything to sell. Unemployment went through the roof in Britain, 4 million, 6 million... 8 million before they stopped counting. The very concept of a job was now a thing of the past. At street level, things became savage very quickly. People became desperate for food and clean water. Families sold their chattels on eBay at first but when the grid went down were forced to barter on street corners selling what little they had of any practical use in order to meet first mortgage payments, then the basic necessities of life. No one wanted their cars, plasma TV sets or iPods, these items were now worthless. Tinned goods became the currency of choice and bottled water acquired a value beyond money.

The loss of household electricity was the most disturbing; a new dark age had begun. It started with power cuts. Because of the freezing weather natural gas was being used up a rate which meant supplies were soon exhausted. Nuclear power could not fill the yawning gap in demand so in the winter of 2021 Britain was blacked out by nationwide power cuts from 7am to 7pm every day. At first the cuts were zonal and the areas scheduled for blackouts were printed in the regional press, just as they had been during the miners' strike in the 1970s. Only this time there was to be no return to normal. At first, what was left of our manufacturing industry was given priority, but as the arctic winter dragged on the government was forced to divert what was left for household consumption. Even so, 12-hour cuts became 18-hour cuts until eventually the lights went out, permanently. Water shortages meant that toilets could not be flushed and the smell of untreated faeces along with household rot was an all-pervasive odour. Now the night became a fearful place in the cities. Feral youth, drunk on pillaged alcohol and armed with clubs and knives, roamed at will, stealing and killing to get what they needed to survive. As the savage winter ended, rubbish remained piled up on the streets and with no more power hospitals were unable to treat the sick, who died in their homes or on the street.

Politics had changed quickly as the reality of the desperate times facing the people of Britain had at last sunk in. In the early years, between 2010 and 2020 there was the calm before the storm. The coming oil shortage and the successive freezing winters had been played down by the spin doctors of a moderate Conservative government. However, after the savage winters of 2019 and 2020, this government was replaced by a new political party, the United Britain Party which had rapidly gained support among the electorate. It was a quasi-fascist organisation supported by the Army and the vast majority of the British people, according to opinion pollsters. Its appeal was to old-fashioned patriotism and support for the monarchy. Its policy was the repatriation of all legal and illegal immigrants who had entered the country since 2000. Although popular, these measures turned out to be impractical and inadequate given the size of the population, now near 70 million and the energy shortages, cruelly exposed by the arctic weather, now a fixture.

By the winter of 2021, new epidemics, untreated and untreatable, raged across the cities during the brief summer thaws. No one knew how many dead or dying there were, a million, maybe more. As bad luck would have it, Britain would freeze while other areas of the globe warmed up. The British public cursed their misfortune but the worst was yet to come. This pattern of cold winters and short summers continued to accelerate, before reaching a peak in 2025 and then gradually tapered off until 2040 when man-made global warming again adjusted the climate of Western Europe and the era of big heat began in Britain.

By then, the former fat-cat bankers and captains of industry were long gone on their private jets, fuelled by the last of the aviation fuel carefully put aside for just such an eventuality. Off to hideaways in New Zealand or Australia, or armed enclaves in California where the population densities were a lot less, and the living easier. Those unfortunates left in the UK were left to face savagery and starvation without the help of the state, and would do so with stoicism and resignation. There was no way out; commercial air travel was long gone, the airlines all bankrupt. The Channel Tunnel had been sealed and anyone who had enough petrol to fill up a car had already got out. Mothers, toddlers, grandmas... there was no escape from the horrors to come in the septic isle of their birth. By 2030, millions had died, and what was left of anything resembling society had been dismantled by an army of scavengers. With no more industry, everything that was once taken for granted and then thrown away was gone. Clothes, tools, medicine, shoes, toothbrushes, toilet paper, soap. There was no manufacturing industry to make these things any more so they became artefacts of a lost age. Those left alive had already sifted through every abandoned home and supermarket for tinned food and bottled water, anything they could use, then after that was all gone through every rubbish tip and landfill for anything they could recycle.

Those who were in possession of tools such as screwdrivers, pliers or saws were rich indeed as these tools were now like gold dust and were used to fix broken shelters, bicycles and the remnants of a lost consumer society. Anyone who could farm or was able to grow fresh produce was also able to survive, but only so long as he watched his back, and carried a gun.

CHAPTER TWO
IT HAPPENED BEFORE, IT WILL HAPPEN AGAIN

Ice cores are like time capsules. They hold within them an incredibly detailed record of Earth's climate. Every year, snow falling on glacial areas accumulates, piling on top of thousands of years of past snow and compacting the snow into layers of ice. Preserved in this ice are tiny bubbles of ancient air that can be analysed, revealing to scientists exactly what was in the atmosphere thousands of years ago.

In 1989, the National Science Foundation funded a huge $25 million project called the Greenland Ice Sheet Project II (GISP2) to drill an ice core right through the entire two-mile depth of the Greenland ice sheet. At the same time, a separate European project called GRIP performed a similar operation, drilling through the ice just 20 miles away.

This second site served as an independent check on

the GISP2 data. By 1993, both the GRIP and GISP2 drills had hit bedrock, and two miles of ice cores preserving 110,000 years of climate history in year-by-year layers were taken to laboratories for analysis.

This was an incredible undertaking but what the scientists found was to prove even more incredible, and troubling. As expected, the ice cores extracted from the Greenland ice sheet were found to have detailed records of ancient air temperatures preserved within them. What was not expected were the results that showed the climate had shifted dramatically several times in very short time spans, time spans as short as a single decade.

Scientists already knew that Earth's climate had been subject to significant fluctuations in the past but what amazed them now was how quickly these changes had taken place. They found out that, over the past 110,000 years, there had been at least 20 abrupt climate changes and that only one relatively stable period had ever existed, the 10,000 years of modern climate we now live in, known as the Holocene period. All of what we know of as human civilisation has existed in this brief and possibly temporary state. (1)

The Earth's climate during the last 2 million years has been dominated by shifts between colder periods, known as Ice Ages or glacials, and warmer periods, known as interglacials. While Ice Ages have tended to last for up to 100,000 years, the intervening interglacial periods have usually been much shorter, at around 10,000 years in length. As stated, during this last interglacial period, all of human civilisation has evolved. As far as we know, the interglacial before the one we have now occurred about 120,000 years ago. We may be coming to the end of this Holocene interglacial but these are the events that led up to it:

THE YOUNGER DRYAS

Around 15,000 years ago, the Earth was beginning to emerge from the last long Ice Age with temperatures starting to approach the levels we have on our planet today. However, just as the ice was finally disappearing, about 13,000 years ago, temperatures suddenly rose in Greenland and the Gulf Stream Conveyor shut down ushering in the Younger Dryas, yet another 1,300 years of freezing conditions. Average temperatures in the North Atlantic region abruptly plummeted nearly 5°C and glacial conditions returned before rapidly warming back again to near-current levels. The weather in Britain during the Younger Dryas was probably similar to that found in Siberia and northern Canada today. Average coastal temperatures would have ranged from -20°C in winter to no more than 10°C (50°F) in summer.

Further inland, it would have been colder still. Pack ice and icebergs would have been seen as far south as Spain, and violent storms and blizzards were a common feature between September and May. Mankind, still at the hunter-gatherer stage, needed to completely change in order to survive. The mammoths they killed for food had all but disappeared as had the fruits and forage early man had found in such abundance. Those humans left alive adopted a new strategy to survive the total absence of food, and became farmers, growing their own food and preserving it for the lean months of winter.

Many of these changes happened rapidly. As the Earth emerged from the final phase of the Younger Dryas, the Greenland ice-core data showed that an 8°C (15°F) warming had occurred in less than a single decade.

No!

THE 8,000-YEAR EVENT

A similar abrupt cooling occurred 8,000 years ago. It was not so severe and lasted only about a century. Many scientists think that it was caused by the bursting of a huge glacial lake followed by a sudden influx of fresh water from North American glaciers. Then, much of what is now central Canada was essentially a giant lake which was prevented from flowing into the Hudson Bay by a wall of enormous ice sheets. However, at around this time, these ice sheets abruptly melted and released a flood of approximately 100,000 cubic kilometres of fresh water as well as thousands of icebergs into the North Atlantic, and this played havoc with ocean currents. Evidence extracted from Greenland ice cores shows that the Greenland ice sheet became 6°C (42.8°F) *No!* colder over this period of time but for us further south the icy blast was felt just as much. In Britain, average temperatures dropped by about 2°C(35.6°F) *No!* and our usual rain belt moved way to the south. Maybe this is beginning to sound familiar. There was an almost instantaneous impact in the North Atlantic, with the conveyor belt system slowing down, stopping warm tropical water flowing north. Temperatures fell dramatically, and stayed low for almost 200 years. This change in the ocean currents was thought to have been enough to shut down ocean circulation and alter global climate. What caused the melting is not known for certain but, if a similar cooling event occurred today, it would be catastrophic. Recent warming of the Greenland ice sheet has allowed melt water to alter the strength of the Gulf Stream which will lead to its slowing within the next ten years and a potentially drastic change in the climate of the British Isles.

THE MEDIEVAL WARM PERIOD (MWP)

An abrupt warming took place about 1,000 years ago. There is evidence of this from a variety of sources such as tree-rings, ice cores and farmers' records in historical documents.

They all suggest that there was a period of great warming between the 9th and 14th centuries when temperatures were higher than they have been for most of the last 200 years in Western Europe.(2)

Reliable evidence for this MWP comes from a 1,100-year tree-ring reconstruction of past summer temperatures in New Zealand, by Cook, Palmer and D'Arrigo, who concluded that 'selected temperature proxies from the Northern and Southern Hemispheres confirm that the MWP was highly variable in time and space. Regardless, the New Zealand temperature reconstruction supports the global occurrence of the MWP.' (3)

There were no accurate measurements of the weather to call upon during this time but the written histories tell us that, from AD 1000 for about 300 years, Greenland flourished, and they record the discovery and colonisation of this then fertile land by legendary Viking Eric the Red. Eric was exiled from Iceland for manslaughter and sailed west, where he discovered Greenland. He then returned briefly and led many ships from Iceland, filled with people who wanted a fresh start on this verdant green land. Over time, they built new communities and traded with other countries and the population increased. At their peak, these settlements became home to several thousand people who were able to farm the land, produce meat and dairy produce, and export goods to Europe; they even built a cathedral. All this activity took place on what is now a sheet of solid ice. But this new community didn't last very long, because around 1325 the climate cooled drastically and the people started to abandon their settlements. Why this happened is uncertain but towards the end of the 14th century there was virtually no sunspot activity recorded for seven decades and subsequently, for 60–70 years between 1000 and 1300, the northern half of our planet was frozen again. In England, the River Thames froze solid and Eric the Red abandoned Greenland when its land again became an icy waste.

The first record of sunspots dates to around 800 BC in China and the oldest surviving drawing of a sunspot dates to 1128 but these do not provide enough data to arrive at any firm conclusions for the causes of Eric's misfortune.

Scientists do not know exactly what caused the warming and melting that triggered the collapses of the remote past. One thing for sure is that it wasn't man-made CO_2. However, data from the ice cores in the Arctic suggest that previous collapses occurred rapidly, often within the space of ten years.

THE LITTLE ICE AGE

The most recent cold spell occurred as recently as the 1700s, known as the Little Ice Age, which was the coldest period in the past 1500 years. Although there is some disagreement over exactly when it started, records of tree-rings and ice cores suggest that temperatures began cooling around 1250 AD. The coldest time was during the 16th and 17th centuries. The time period between 1400 and 1900 recorded the lowest average global temperatures, specifically low at around 1450, 1650 and 1820. This first Little Ice Age gave an early indication of a connection between Earth's climate and the action of the sun. The Spörer minimum was a 90-year period, from about 1460 until 1550 notable for a complete dearth of sunspots. It occurred before sunspots had ever been observed, and was discovered later by analysis of the proportion of carbon-14 in tree-rings which is strongly correlated with solar activity, as we shall see later.

Each period was separated by slight warming intervals, the same kind of weather we have now. In the Far East, history tells us that in the 13th century the Mongolians suffered a terrible drought which led them to invade China in a search of food.

Temperature declines elsewhere were followed by wars, famines and population reductions. Another dearth of sunspots occurred during the Maunder minimum of 1645–1715 at the time of another little ice age on Earth. This was the time of the Great Famine and The Black Death in Western Europe when those who were fortunate enough to live past the age of 30 were considered to be really old.

Between 1400 and 1850, severe winters had profound agricultural, economic and political impacts. Cooling caused glaciers to advance and stunted tree growth. This was a time of cooler climate in most areas of the world, not just northern Europe.

During the Little Ice Ages, average global temperatures were 1–1.5°C (33.8–34.7°F) less than they are today. The best guess is that cooler temperatures over this shorter time scale were caused by a combination of less solar activity and large volcanic eruptions, including the Tambora eruption.

No!

This eruption is the worst volcano disaster in recorded history. On 10 April 1815, Mount Tambora in Indonesia blew its top and killed 10,000 people from the explosion and another 82,000 people from related starvation and disease. The mountain, which stood 13,000 feet tall, was reduced in height by 4,000 feet after blasting 93 cubic miles of ash into the atmosphere, blocking the sun's rays and significantly cooling the globe. Snow fell in the north-east coast of America from June to August that year and caused widespread crop failures and famine, both in America and Europe. In turn, this led to what became known as 'the year without summer' of 1816. Livestock died, harvests failed, Britons saw Eskimos paddling canoes in their coastal waters. Winters were longer and growing seasons shorter. The wet weather caused terrible related diseases such as the bubonic plague as people moved around in search of salvation. Epidemics may not be directly linked to temperature change, but mass migration creates the ideal scenario for diseases to spread.

Many rivers flooded due to higher than normal rainfall and it is estimated that 200,000 people died in eastern and southern Europe from hunger and a typhus epidemic. Southern India suffered a cholera epidemic. Farms and villages in northern Europe were deserted because the farmers couldn't grow crops in the cooler climate and food was so short that bread had to be made from the bark of trees when grains would no longer grow. The crop failure in America caused farmers to move westwards and this mass migration shifted the nation's farming industry away from the eastern part of the USA to the mid-western Corn Belt.

Eastern Canada experienced the same weather

conditions with cold waves, frost and drought. Sub-zero temperatures killed crops and at least a foot of snow fell in Quebec City in early June. The crops that managed to survive were killed by early frost in September.

In Britain, the eruption brought on the third coldest summer since record-keeping began in 1659. Freezing temperatures and prolonged rain caused massive crop failures in France as well as Britain, Switzerland and Germany. Europe, already suffering from food shortages due to the Napoleonic Wars, was plagued by riots and looting. In Asia and India, they experienced unusually low temperatures and frost. Rice production fell drastically which resulted in famine in China.

By 1850, the climate started to warm up again bringing an end to decades of misery.

What is significant about these historical records is that they form the most likely template for what will happen again in Britain, Western Europe and North America between 2020 and 2040. We're heading for the 30 coldest winters we've had in nearly 200 years.

An organisation with no obvious political axe to grind is the Woods Hole Oceanographic Institution (WHOI), a private, non-profit research and higher-education facility dedicated to the study of marine science and engineering and to the education of marine researchers. Established in 1930, it is the largest independent oceanographic research institution in the US, with staff and students numbering about 1,000 and is the foremost authority on climate change in the US.

In 2003, Robert B. Gagosian, President and Director of WHOI, delivered a lecture to the World Economic Forum, in which he stated:

If cold, salty North Atlantic waters did not sink, a primary force driving global ocean circulation could slacken and cease. Existing currents could weaken or be redirected. The resulting reorganization of the ocean's circulation would reconfigure Earth's climate patterns.

Computer models simulating ocean-atmosphere climate dynamics indicate that the North Atlantic region would cool 3° to 5° Celsius if Conveyor circulation were totally disrupted. It would produce winters twice as cold as the worst winters on record in the eastern United States in the past century. In addition, previous Conveyor shutdowns have been linked with widespread droughts throughout the globe. It is crucial to remember two points: 1) If thermohaline circulation shuts down and induces a climate transition, severe winters in the

North Atlantic region would likely persist for decades to centuries – until conditions reached another threshold at which thermohaline circulation might resume. 2) Abrupt regional cooling may occur even as the Earth, on average, continues to warm.

If the climate system's Achilles' heel is the Conveyor, the Conveyor's Achilles' heel is the North Atlantic. An influx of fresh water into the North Atlantic's surface could create a lid of more buoyant fresh water, lying atop denser, saltier water. This fresh water would effectively cap and insulate the surface of the North Atlantic, curtailing the ocean's transfer of heat to the atmosphere.

An influx of fresh water would also dilute the North Atlantic's salinity. At a critical but unknown threshold, when North Atlantic waters are no longer sufficiently salty and dense, they may stop sinking. An important force driving the Conveyor could quickly diminish, with climate impacts resulting within a decade. (4)

This whole area of research into ocean circulation patterns is both new and complicated but more than one eminent scientist believes a Gulf Stream slowdown appears the most likely outcome for the UK.

It was a professor from the National Oceanography Centre in Southampton who would shock the world of climatology and the media with the surprising results of his research. On 30 November 2005, Professor Harry Bryden's findings were carried on TheNewScientist.com news service. Bryden's research team had found a 30 per cent reduction in the warm currents that carry water north from the Gulf Stream. Bryden was cagey about the data presented. 'We don't want to say the circulation will shut down,' he said. 'But we are nervous about our findings.' (5)

His team had measured the flow of heat from north to south in 2004 using a string of temperature-sensitive data recorders placed from the Canary Islands to the Bahamas. They found that the crucial division of the waters flowing north had changed dramatically since their previous surveys conducted in 1957, 1981 and 1992. They looked at the volume of water in the subtropical gyre and its flow southwards at depth and made the calculation that north-flowing warm water had decreased by 30 per cent.

Many scientists were sceptical about this early research. MIT oceanographer Carl Wunch compared Bryden's methodology to 'measuring temperatures in Hamburg on five random days and then concluding that the climate is getting warmer or cooler'.

Wallace Broecker of Columbia University, and the

man who had first suggested that Gulf Stream shutdowns could explain historical climatic changes, wrote to *Science* magazine, criticising Bryden et al of making claims that will 'only intensify the existing polarization over global warming'.(6)

Broecker argued that a global-warming-induced abrupt climate change is not likely to happen for at least 100 years in the future, by which time Earth's temperature will have warmed enough to offset the abrupt cooling a circulation shutdown would trigger.

In February 2009, in response to this criticism, Bryden stated:

With respect to the 2005 *Nature* article about the overturning circulation slowing down, we have since analysed all the historical observations we could find from the region of 25°N. I think the evidence is that the overturning slowed down by 2 to 4 Sv (defined as 1 million cubic metres per second) since 1980, or about 15% since 1980 compared with our conclusion of a 30% slowdown since 1957 as stated in the *Nature* article. We submitted a scientific article on our results to *Journal of Physical Oceanography* in October 2007 and we are awaiting a decision from the editor as to whether it will be accepted for publication. My science is oriented towards observing the overturning, we have a NERC-funded Rapid project to monitor the Atlantic overturning at 25°N through 2014 and I am most interested to see what the variability in the overturning is: are there large inter-annual changes, a trend, a sudden jump, or no change at all. Criticism is always tough to take but that is how science works: new findings are seldom overwhelmingly conclusive, so they are generally controversial and undergo substantial criticism and review, as they should. (7)

So the Gulf Stream is slowing down, but at half the catastrophic rate first predicted by Bryden et al. The result of this will still be longer, colder winters and shorter summers from around 2019 but the good news is that this pattern of events may last for a less protracted period of time, until about 2040, before we begin to get warmer. Computer models are just not sophisticated enough yet to give us exact dates.

We need to rely on accumulated evidence, and indeed more evidence of the Gulf Stream slowing has come from a professor of ocean physics at Cambridge University.

Professor Peter Wadhams began hitching rides under the North Polar ice cap on the Navy sub *HMS Tireless* in 1996. At first, his aim was to measure the thickness of the ice from underneath to find out if it was shrinking due to global warming. Over the past 20 years, his surveys have revealed a 46 per cent reduction in the thickness of the ice. It was the results of Wadhams' research that caused the scientific community to take a collective gulp. Wadhams had been below the Arctic ice sheet measuring the dense cold water chimneys which sink to the sea bed to be replaced by warm water. These chimneys, normally there are 12 of them, are the engines that drive the North Atlantic Drift, our climatic lifeline in winter. Wadhams found that the chimneys had all but disappeared. There remained only two giant columns of sinking water, both significantly weakened.

Wadhams confirmed, 'Until recently we would find giant "chimneys" in the sea where columns of cold, dense water were sinking from the surface to the seabed 3,000 metres below, but now they have almost disappeared. As the water sank, it was replaced by warm water flowing in from the south which kept the circulation going. If that mechanism is slowing it will mean less heat reaching Europe.'

As of January 2009, Wadhams has had his last ten grant applications turned down by the government's Natural Environment Research Council (NERC). This includes work on the disappearance of the giant whirlpools off Greenland that may point to a slowing down or shutdown of the Gulf Stream. An explosion aboard *HMS Tireless* in 2008 nearly cost Peter Wadhams his life. He survived when the damaged sub punched up through the wafer thin ice to the surface. But what really concerns Wadhams is his belief that the government and NERC are preventing his research work continuing. 'NERC is constantly saying in its publicity that sea ice is a critical parameter of climate change. But it won't provide me with any funding, even though the submarines are being provided free of charge. I am the most experienced Arctic researcher in Britain so I have to conclude that it is personal.' (8)

In 2007, the IPCC Fourth Assessment Report Summary for Policymakers gave a summary of the results of a number of computing models that had made separate predictions as to the likely average temperature of the world in 2100. The report, presented to the UN, looked at a number of different scenarios where the concentration of greenhouse gases in the atmosphere was seen to change over time. The worst-case scenario showed what would happen if no action was taken to reduce greenhouse-gas emissions. Here carbon dioxide levels in the atmosphere reached 1550 parts per million (ppm) by 2100. At the other end of the scale, the concentration of CO_2 could be reduced to 600ppm. Strangely, the

IPCC found that with either course of action – doing a lot, or doing nothing to curb greenhouse-gas emissions – the temperature of the world would stay about how it is now until 2030. Some parts of the world would warm up a little, while others would cool a little. However, after 2030, there is a marked divergence with the lower-emission scenario seeing temperatures increase by 1.8°C (35.2°F) by 2100 and with the 'do nothing' scenario by 4°C (39.2°F). That's what we can expect by the end of the century. This is the bottom line. We can do nothing and continue to burn all the rest of our fossil fuels and we'll still be here at the end of this century. The world will be hotter, the climate will be more unpredictable and population in the developing nations will be through the roof. For industrialists, bankers and the movers and shakers of the capitalist system life will go on as normal until at least 2020, the business-as-usual scenario of the last 100 years. This is the mindset of what the author Tom Wolfe termed the 'masters of the universe' and they are unlikely to loosen their grip on the reins of industrial and economic power without real persuasion.

The IPCC also told the UN that they were 90–99 per cent certain that the MOC of the Atlantic Ocean will slow down during the 21st century. For most of the world's scientific community and those who believe in man-made global warming, the words of James Lovelock, former NASA scientist and Gaia guru, are climate gospel. Lovelock also believes that Britain may freeze before it fries. He has stated,

> I can't help wondering if the climate of the British Isles and the western part of northern Europe, which is now 8°C warmer than the same latitudes in other parts of the world, may be largely unchanged by global heating, because the 8°C lost when the Gulf Stream fails is just about equal to the predicted rise of temperature from global heating.' (9)

That is going to affect all of us in Britain and we need to get ready; we may have less than ten years to prepare for a fundamental change in our climate no one is expecting.

CHAPTER THREE
2025: THE STATE WE'RE IN

It seems like only yesterday that scientists were predicting a new ice age in the press and on television. When I was at school in the 1970s, I remember watching a BBC documentary telling us about a seemingly fundamental change in the world's weather.

The same was true in America. This is what Peter Gwynne wrote for *Newsweek* on 28 April 1975: 'There are ominous signs that the Earth's weather patterns have begun to change dramatically and that these changes may portend a drastic decline in food production with serious political implications for just about every nation on Earth.'

There was no drop in food production and no ice age. Since 1975, the tide of opinion reversed dramatically and scientists began to be worried about what man-made global warming and its effects were doing to the planet. What would happen if global warming were to cause the west Antarctic ice sheet, some 3.8 million cubic kilometres of ice, to break up and slide into the ocean? Is there ever any firm consensus about what's happening to the Earth's climate?

Scientific minds have lately become focused on what has become the generally accepted cause of our climatic problems, the greenhouse effect. This is the rise in temperature the Earth experiences because certain gases present in the atmosphere like water vapour, carbon dioxide and methane are able to contain or trap radiated energy from the sun after it hits the surface of our planet. Put simply, solar energy enters our atmosphere on a wavelength short enough to allow it to pass through the greenhouse-gas blanket which envelops our planet. These rays are absorbed by the Earth then reflected back into space at a different, longer heat wavelength. Greenhouse gases trap some of this reflected heat in the lower atmosphere, but most of the heat escapes back into space. Without these gases, all of the heat would be completely lost and Earth's temperature would be a lot colder, making it, over a relatively short period of time, like a giant ball of ice. These greenhouse gases warm our world, but, if their concentrations increase, more of the reflected heat is captured in the lower atmosphere and this causes temperatures at the surface of the Earth to rise.

As it works now, this carbon exchange, beginning in outer space and ending on planet Earth, is a life-giving miracle, a tightrope act on a cosmic scale, this movement of carbon through our atmosphere. On land and sea plants all the colours of the rainbow drink in carbon in order to make their food then release it in a different form at night, as oxygen. Trees, some of which can live for hundreds of years, store away vast amounts of this carbon, as do the world's oceans, which store more carbon than exits in the Earth's atmosphere as a whole. This vast recycling factory allows humanity to thrive, giving us our food and water and the air we breathe. The Green argument, and the one now adopted by some world leaders, is that one of the gases present in the lower atmosphere, carbon dioxide, is becoming too prevalent, trapping too much heat and is starting to melt the ice caps. Also, the burning of fossil fuels, largely to power the motor car, means that we're adding an extra 7 billion tonnes of carbon to our atmosphere each year. Although this amounts to a small fraction of the carbon already up there, the worry is that a significant percentage of this extra carbon, some say 50 per cent, is not being reabsorbed and is building up year on year to a point where the Earth is becoming too hot. The Green movement is convinced that carbon dioxide emissions must peak by 2015 if we are not to suffer the consequences of a 2°C (35.6°F) warming of the Earth's atmosphere and a possible 'runaway greenhouse effect'.

The IPCC has estimated that a collapse of the West Antarctic ice sheet would raise sea levels around the world by about 17 feet on average. In 2007 research from the IPCC's fourth report showed that if this ice sheet completely melted, the east coast of North America would experience a rise in sea levels more than four feet higher than had been previously predicted, of nearer 21 feet, enough to submerge New York City. The IPCC predicts that most of Europe would have sea-level rises of about 18 feet and nations near the southern Indian Ocean, like Bangladesh, would see their coastal areas completely flooded.

The result of this huge rise in sea levels would not only be a displacement of the world's poorer peoples, there would be other consequences such as higher rates of coastal erosion, greater storm damage and problems with the polluted ocean contaminating groundwater drinking supplies.

Aside from vast areas of America's Gulf States, including Miami, other areas under threat of complete obliteration would be Brazil, Burma and Holland. Low-lying cities such as Venice, New Orleans and London would disappear beneath the waves. One of the first casualties of future weather-related catastrophe is likely to be the insurance industries, which look unlikely to survive the 21st century in their current incarnations. Hurricane Andrew which swept over Florida in 1992 (missing Miami) was enough to bankrupt several large insurance companies and the backwash was a refusal of those companies left standing to insure the Caribbean Islands against any future hurricanes. In 2005, the year of Hurricane Katrina, industry losses racked up to over $200 billion.

The insurance industry needs to worry about its future prospects. The 2007 IPCC Fourth Assessment Report Summary for policymakers states that, based on current model simulations, it is very likely that the MOC of the Atlantic Ocean will slow down during the 21st century.

In sciencespeak, 'very likely' means it is 90–99 per cent certain that this event will occur. As we have seen, a shutdown of the MOC would suddenly decrease the amount of heat in the North Atlantic, leading to much colder temperatures in Europe and North America. The possible freezing of the UK and Europe will depend on the amount of greenhouse gases in the atmosphere and the speed with which the MOC slows down. It's not a case of *if* this event will happen, only of *when*. Global warming will increase the melting of the Greenland ice sheet and the melting of polar sea ice will increase the amount of fresh water flowing into the critical deep-water formation zones near Greenland.

A 2005 comparison of 11 climate models showed that the MOC is likely to slow by 10–50 per cent whatever happens because levels of carbon dioxide are now so elevated. In the long run, any cooling caused by the MOC slowing would be offset by the increase in greenhouse gases that would reheat Britain after 2040, but that's in the long run. In the short term, Britain will suffer very cold winters.

The historical records show that abrupt climate change is not only probable but that it's the normal state of affairs. The present warm, stable climate we live in is the anomaly. What happens to water levels may turn out to be a bit more complicated than the IPCC reports suggest. Rising sea levels cannot just be attributed to melting glaciers without taking into account the thermal expansion of water as it heats up, and that must take into account the action of the sun.

Changes in temperature invariably lead to increases in demand for energy, to keep warm or to cool off. What worries many economists is the huge rise in the demand for oil predicted by those who fear the worst is yet to come. The Energy Information Agency (EIA) report of 2009 predicted that world demand for oil would increase by 37 per cent (from 2006 levels) up to 2030. That's a jump from 86 million barrels a day to 118 million barrels a day. Bear in mind this is the rate of increase, not what we already use up on a daily basis.

When we see the first major global industry collapse completely because of high oil prices, we will know that, despite any government assurances given, the full-blown energy crisis is upon us. Beating the insurance industry to that dubious finishing line will undoubtedly be the airline industry.

Oil provides 90 per cent of our transportation energy and the cost of aviation fuel has more than doubled since the beginning of 2004.

The profitability of airlines is coming under increasing pressure because of competition and overcapacity. This, and their other major headache, terrorism, has had negative effects on demand while the cost of airport security has soared.

On 20 January 2010, Japan Airlines announced it had filed for bankruptcy with a third of its workforce to be laid off immediately, some 15,600 jobs. All of the company's directors immediately resigned. On hearing this news, the world's stock markets devalued the airline's shares to little more than junk, about $150 million in total, less than the cost of one brand-new jumbo jet. This is one of Japan's biggest ever corporate failures, but it's not the only airline in a tailspin. Also in deep trouble is US flagship carrier American Airlines, who have been forced to cut routes as a result of the high cost of fuel and Northwest Airlines, whose shares dropped from $22 to less than $4 in a 12-month period. Ryanair and easyJet have managed to stay profitable by cannily managing to fix or hedge the price that they pay for aviation fuel (Ryanair at $45, easyJet at $60). But eventually even this fixed rate price will expire.

Within the next ten years, the rate of worldwide oil extraction will be unable to meet demand and fuel prices will rocket. Weaker airlines without hedging contracts will be the first to go as higher fuel costs kill off the competitive advantage they once had and the airline industry will collapse, almost overnight. Maybe the last to go will be the flag carriers from the Middle East, like Emirates, as this will be the only region to benefit from the high oil prices. Emirates have recently ordered 45 new Airbus A380s; they can keep going until at least the middle of the next decade, but they will be the last of the commercial carriers. As oil prices continue to rise, the world economy will be plunged into a deep depression with an accompanying increase in inflation and there will be massive disruption to air transportation. By the middle of this century the air industry will have disappeared and those privileged view who can fly will either be rich beyond measure or high-ranking government officials.

This situation should come as no surprise to the airlines. They were warned many years ago that oil couldn't last forever by Dr Marion King Hubbert.

The man known as King Hubbert was born in Texas in 1903. He gained a PhD in geology and physics in 1937 at the University of Chicago and then taught geophysics at Columbia University until 1941 before becoming a research geophysicist with the Shell Oil Company. In 1948, Hubbert predicted that for any given geographical area the rate of petroleum production over time would resemble a bell curve. This became known as the 'Hubbert Curve'. His prediction that US oil production would peak in 1970 proved to be correct. In 1974, Hubbert stated that 'if current trends continue' global oil production would peak in 1995. After the effects of the OPEC oil embargo of 1973 were extrapolated, he modified this prediction to say that the effect of this embargo would delay the peak by a decade. That makes the date of worldwide peak production 2005, a date many within the oil industry now quietly accept as fact.

Richard Heinberg's book *The Party's Over* makes it clear the fossil-fuel bonanza is well and truly over. He says:

The work of Hubbert and his followers is based on far better data and a far more robust understanding of the process of oil depletion than was available in the 20th century. Hubbert predicted that US oil production would peak in 1970; it did. By now, roughly two dozen oil producing nations have passed their all-time production peaks. Nearly every year, another nation joins the "past-peak club". Thus the discussion of the phenomenon of peak oil is as much about history as it is about prediction. The degree of extrapolation needed narrows with each passing year. Why was there apparently more oil in the ground in 1956 than there was in 1955? Because these were some of the best years in history for oil discovery worldwide. Discovery rates have fallen off dramatically since then. The rate of discovery of new oil in the lower-48 US peaked in the 1930s; discovery worldwide peaked in the 1960s. Today, in a typical year, we are pumping and burning between five and six barrels of oil for each new barrel discovered. Demand for oil continues to increase, on average, at about two percent per year. From such an estimate it should be possible to derive a working estimate of when global demand for oil will exceed supply. (1)

If 2005 was the year of global peak oil, working from Heinberg's detailed analysis (he believes world oil production peaked in 2003), we can derive an estimate that worldwide oil production in 2030 will be about the same as it was in 1980. The problem is that the world's population in 2030 will be approximately double its current size, more industrialised and therefore more oil-dependent than it was in 1980.

It is an absolute certainty that, in the absence of enough renewables to fill the yawning gap, the price of oil will reach stratospheric levels before industrial civilisation begins to topple.

Western economies, dependent on a continuous flow of oil, will be slowly parched and in the ensuing panic to preserve what's left, wars fought over remaining reserves are a real possibility.

Again, given these figures, the awful load of excess population comes to bear down. Heinberg warns:

Expanding agricultural production, based on cheap energy resources, enabled the feeding of a global population that grew from 1.7 billion to over 6 billion people in a single century. Cheap oil energy will soon be a thing of the past. How many people will post-industrial agriculture be able to support? This is an extremely important question, but one that is difficult to answer. A safe estimate would be this: as many people as were supported before agriculture was industrialised – that is, the population at the beginning of the 20th century, or somewhat fewer than 2 billion. (2)

Those economists who think the market will come up with a last-gasp solution to this crisis are in denial. The goals all nations of the developed and developing world have given themselves, to constantly increase their incomes and GDP, are no longer attainable. As China continues to industrialise, it will require around 99 million barrels of oil per day by 2031. The total world production of oil in 2009 was only 84 million barrels per day. It doesn't take a genius to work out that even present levels of world industrial production and consumption of oil are unsustainable. The false hope of traditional Keynesian economists that government stimulation of the market will allow us to come up with some miracle technological fix, like fusion power, ignores the real situation. We simply don't have the long lead-in times required for any alternative energy or renewable energy projects to get up and running before we run out of fossil fuels, or the billions needed to change to a new energy infrastructure to accommodate new energy sources.

What we can do is ameliorate the worst effects of the coming crisis by taking action immediately. Globalisation must be consigned to the pages of history and we need to bring in regulations to restrict economic growth and the all-out consumption of fossil fuels. Only this will buy us the time to make the transition to a post fossil-fuel era. Looking at the evidence, you begin to be struck by an awful historical symmetry that seems to be unfolding. The early years of the last century, the Edwardian era, up to the outbreak of the Great War were peaceful. The years after the end of the war were prone to economic turmoil, decadence and, finally, complete financial collapse, leading to the emergence of authoritarian governments, the rise of fascism and then another world war. Could the 21st century be following a similar pattern? If all the oil is gone by 2040, it is well within the realms of possibility that running up to this date the current period of relative calm could be replaced by economic chaos brought on by climate change in the 2020s, authoritarian government in the 2030s, then a shorter lead-in to horrific resource wars soon after as the last industrialised nations battle for control of dwindling oil resources. Man is still a tribal species with Stone Age instincts. The veneer of civilisation we have developed over a few hundred years won't prevent the aggressive instincts forged over a million from quickly resurfacing in savagery when the system starts to break down. Look no further than the 20th century, the most violent in our recorded history. The nation they said was the most civilised on Earth murdered 6 million Jews, within living memory.

As Heinberg points out, there is nothing that can fill the oil gap, no amount of renewables or conservation can save industrial civilisation, not with population levels as they are.

The fragility of the world's economies, deprived of their fossil-fuel lifeblood, will see the return of mass unemployment and this will change the political arena. The lessons of recent history should not be forgotten. In the winter of 1932, there were 6 million people out of work in Germany, 30 per cent of the workforce. Industry had been devastated by world economic depression after the Wall Street Crash of 1929 and Hitler's minister of economics Hjalmar Schacht pumped huge amounts of money into the economy in an effort to create demand and work. These were similar measures Gordon Brown's government introduced to the British economy in 2009 under the banner of 'quantitative easing'.

In Germany, the stimulus paid for the autobahns and the enlargement of the armed forces. Prices and wages were controlled and taxes increased. These essentially Keynesian solutions were financed by printing new money. Three years later, unemployment in Germany was under 1 million but the country was being run by Adolf Hitler as a totalitarian state where democracy was demolished and the workforce controlled by brute force and repression.

The banking collapses in Britain and elsewhere in Europe have already had a knock-on effect in the political arena. The crisis is not over, and will come back to haunt Britain when Eastern Europe, submerged in a mountain of debt that it can't repay, asks for more money from the EU, which the EU can no longer afford to dole out.

Latvia, for instance, has been burdened with a debt far beyond its ability to pay. Its mortgages have mostly been taken out in foreign currency, so Latvia cannot even inflate its way out of trouble. Nor will it help for the government to borrow from the IMF and EU to pay the debts of its insolvent real estate to other foreign banks. Public-sector borrowing to bail out bad private-sector debts means squeezing the money out of the Latvian population by higher taxes, thereby pricing it and its industry out of world markets. In this situation, the economy is unable to earn enough to cover its imports and the debts it has been burdened with.

In December 2008, the IMF and EU did agree to bail out bankrupt Latvia to the tune of €7.5 billion in loans. As part of the loan agreement, public-sector wages had to be slashed by 15 per cent in 2009 alongside deep cuts to government expenditure amounting to 10 per cent of Latvia's GDP. In January, there were riots in the Latvian capital in protest against the new austerity. Days later violent protests shook the Bulgarian capital Sofia, also in financial meltdown, and in Lithuania police were called in to disperse some 7,000 demonstrators with tear gas and rubber-tipped bullets. These protests denounced public-sector wage cuts and increases in taxes aimed at aiding these nations' ruined economies. In Latvia, 86 individuals were arrested and Prime Minister Andrius Kubilius was forced to call an emergency cabinet meeting, his country on a knife-edge.

And it's not just Latvia. Lithuania, Bulgaria, Hungary and the Ukraine are effectively bankrupt, the prosperity in the East in recent years having been built on nothing more than a mountain of debt. Alarm bells are also beginning to ring in Austria, Italy and

Scandinavia. All these countries have banks that are heavily exposed in Eastern Europe.

Spain now faces the worst economic crisis in its history as the full effects of the property crash spread through its economy. Even before the global financial crisis of September 2008, Spain was in deep trouble. It reported a GDP budget deficit of 3.8 per cent in 2008, which was mostly due to property-firm failures and the collapse of the construction industry. European Central Bank monetary policy rules prevent Spain from printing money like the US or the UK, and in January 2009 Standard and Poor's downgraded Spain's credit rating from AAA. The downgrade will make it very difficult for Spain to borrow any more, as it increases the price Spain will have to pay for its debt on the international bond market. In April 2009, Spain's top banker Miguel Angel Fernandez Ordonez warned that the country's social-security system would run into deficit within a year unless the government agreed to control public spending.

Iceland's banking system effectively collapsed in October 2008. Since then, Iceland has been struggling to come to terms with creditors trying to recoup the $80 billion they have lost. This crisis saw Iceland's credit rating cut to junk and it is now relying on a $2.1 billion loan from the IMF and a $2.5 billion loan from other Nordic countries to help bail it out. On 5

January 2010, President Olafur R. Grimsson vetoed a UK and Dutch depositor bill after receiving a petition from more than 60,000 of Iceland's 320,000 inhabitants urging him to reject the legislation. The accord, which obliges Iceland to use $5.5 billion in borrowed money to cover the depositor claims, will now be put to a referendum. Polls show about 70 per cent of Icelanders oppose the legislation.

Greece and Ireland were put on credit watch in January 2010 by Standard & Poor's, followed by Portugal and Spain. Greece's sovereign credit rating had been downgraded from A to A minus after it had been found out playing fast and loose with its financial statistics by the European Commission who revealed a budget deficit that had ballooned to 12.7 per cent of its national income. Greece was effectively bust and its socialist government led by George Papandreou was forced to introduce emergency austerity measures in February 2010, including a freeze on public sector pay, an increase in petrol prices and the raising of the retirement age in the hope of attracting a short-term bail-out from German bankers. The hope was to slash the deficit from 12 per cent of GDP to three per cent by 2012. The result was a national strike of public sector workers on February 10, 2010. Who will be the next to default? The Euro is on the verge of meltdown and the banking system teeters on a precipice, another crisis could see a domino effect of defaults and Europe's financial edifice come tumbling down, leading to a crisis far worse than the credit crunch.

From economic chaos comes social unrest. Already there are reports of nationalists in Hungary renewing persecution of Romany communities. Gypsies make up about 7 per cent of the Hungarian population. In February 2009, Romanian handball star Marian Cozma was fatally stabbed at a Hungarian nightclub. At his memorial service, some in the crowd shouted 'Death to the gypsies!' and anti-gypsy demonstrations erupted throughout the country.

The right-wing opposition party, Fidesz, used the stabbing as an opportunity to call on the governing socialist party to clamp down on gypsy communities. A police chief who blamed gypsies for 'all the muggings' in his city, and added, 'Hungarian and gypsy culture can't live together,' was fired by the government, but reinstated within 24 hours after more than 1,000 people protested at a skinhead rally.

Elsewhere in Europe, there has been a renewal of anti-Semitic violence on an unprecedented scale. Most alarming is the potential return of Mussolini-style fascism in Italy. In October 2007, Giovanni Reggiani, a religious education teacher and wife of an Italian naval officer, was brutally murdered by a Romanian gypsy. Her face beaten to a bloody pulp, she was then sexually assaulted and robbed before she died of her wounds. Her murder caused outrage among the voters of Italy's capital city and helped lead to the election of Gianni Alemanno as mayor of Rome in 2008, the first right-wing mayor since Mussolini's era. Thousands of Italians rushed to form vigilante groups, the Italian National Guard, with uniforms featuring Nazi-style armbands, black eagle insignia and black gloves. Since 2007, Silvio Berlusconi's government has brought in laws aimed at fingerprinting the nation's entire population of Roma gypsies and has declared a 'Roma emergency'. The atmosphere in many Italian cities has become toxic. In the small town of Ardo, the mayor posted a reward of 500 euros for anyone reporting an illegal immigrant. Native Italians are becoming increasingly concerned about the constant flood of illegal immigrants from Africa who enter Italy from Libya.

The backlash there has already begun, Britain may well be about to follow. In September 2009, in Harrow a right-wing organisation calling itself The English Defence League tried to protest against what it called the 'Islamification of Europe' by Muslim fanatics. They were hemmed in by the police for their own safety and attacked by hundreds of Muslim protesters.

For people in Greece, though, the announcement of the Secretary for Home Affairs Theodora Tzakri two weeks later, which made clear that Greek citizenship would be granted only to children born to legal immigrants, came as no surprise.

Enoch Powell's infamous 'Rivers of Blood' speech in 1968 quoted the Registrar-General's statistics that in 15 to 20 years time there would be 3.5 million immigrants and their descendants in Britain. Powell estimated that by the year 2000 that figure would be between 5 to 7 million. Powell's rant may have left a bad taste in the mouth but his predictions were not far wrong. According to MigrationwatchUK, net foreign immigration for the year 2005 reached 292,000 and although in 2009 this figure went down to around 250,000 that's one new arrival into Britain every minute. Since 1997 more than three million immigrants have arrived in Britain, 2.67 million officially and 725,000 illegally. Research from a cross-party parliamentary group on immigration co-chaired by former Labour minister Frank Field showed that the population of the UK will reach 70 million by 2028 unless immigration falls by 190,000 a year between now and then. In 2009, official statistics showed there were 250,000 new immigrants entering Britain each year, five times as many as entered the country in 1997. The independent Office for National Statistics (ONS) says that the population of England will increase by 10 million over the next 24 years, and 70 per cent of this increase will be due to immigration

Field explained, 'We cannot afford to let our population grow at the extraordinary pace now officially forecast. The pressures on our public services and communities would be too great to bear.' (3).

According to official government projections, immigration will result in a UK population increase of 6 million up to 2031. That's a more conservative figure than the one supplied by Field's all-party group but is still six times the population of Birmingham. Immigrants and their descendants will account for 83 per cent of future population growth in the UK and that does not include illegal immigrants.

About 50,000 illegal entrants are detected every year. In 2009, a report by the London School of Economics commissioned by the Mayor's Office in London put the total number of illegal immigrants in Britain at 725,000 in 2007. The study found the number of illegal immigrants nationally had risen by nearly 300,000 in six years. Previous estimates in 2001 put the number of illegal immigrants in Britain at about 430,000. Legal immigration at the present projected rate will lead to the need for about 1.5 million new houses in the period 2003–2026 and a need to concrete over vast swathes of Britain's once green and pleasant land.

The rumblings of discontent over allocation of resources, housing and jobs is already growing. In 2009, Labour Immigration Minister Phil Woolas was reported advising the electorate that, if they weren't supporting Labour, to 'go out and vote for one of the other main parties' rather than stay at home, which would possibly result in the BNP winning an MEP seat in the upcoming European Parliamentary elections. Well might he panic, because under New Labour claiming asylum has became the open door to a permanent stay in Britain. Labour's bedrock supporters, the English working class, had committed the cardinal sin of voting for Mrs Thatcher's Conservative party throughout the 1980s.

Rather than trust to a return to traditional voting patterns, New Labour strategists decided instead to import a whole new sector of Labour voters from abroad. They would be doubly beholden to a Labour government who let them settle here in the first place and then gave them jobs in the public sector. Naturally, those without jobs would not want to lose their generous welfare benefits or their new homes. Hey Presto, thought New Labour strategists, no more right-wing Tory governments, ever. Unfortunately, this scenario depended on a constantly growing economy.

Gordon Brown's promise of 'no more boom and bust' was exposed by the banking crash of 2008 and Britain now finds itself having to support hundreds of thousands of legal and illegal immigrants who have little chance of ever finding work in Britain again, but who will fight tooth and nail to remain here.

The magnitude of New Labour's error has begun to cause alarm among those running the government who are wondering how we are to pay for all these economic refugees. The chancellor's April 2009 budget revealed that Britain's national debt will reach £1.7 trillion, equivalent to almost 80 per cent of the nation's GDP. That's 80 per cent of everything produced by every factory and worker in the country. The unprecedented borrowing programme means that a generation of British workers will have to face higher taxes in order to pay off the debt, and raises doubts about international investors' willingness to go on lending to UK plc.

It could be even worse than forecast, since Mr Darling has based his borrowing plans on an assumption that the UK economy will be booming again by 2011, an assumption most fiscal analysts believe to be overly optimistic. Figures published on 26 January, 2010 showed Britain limping out of recession with a growth rate of 0.1 per cent, well below official forecasts of 0.4 per cent.

Budget projections say that public-sector net debt, the amount of outstanding government borrowing, will reach £1,370 billion in 2013/14. When Labour took office in 1997, debt was £350 billion. What happens when Britain's dwindling resources are called upon to cope with a climate-change crisis? Suddenly the allocation of scarce resources becomes a political nightmare that makes the 'British Jobs for British Workers' protest of 2009 look tame.

The penny seems to have dropped too late for New Labour and in recent years over 60 per cent of new asylum seekers have been refused permission to stay in Britain. However, only one in four of those who fail to be granted asylum are ever removed. Health concerns over those who arrive from Africa only make matters more complicated. Health Protection Agency figures showed a 20 per cent increase in new HIV diagnoses in the year to 2003, with around 4,300 new cases being transmitted heterosexually, and most of these infections originating from Africa and mainly from Zimbabwe. African women are being treated in the UK at twice the rate of African men, probably because antenatal testing is now routine in the UK.

In 2004, Health Protection Agency (HPA) figures showed that there were between 28,000 and 30,000 Zimbabweans living in the United Kingdom, at least 10,000 of them living in London. In that year, of all the cases of HIV reported in England and Wales, 25 per cent of the diagnoses were from people of African origin, though they make up less than 1 per cent of the population. According to HPA statistics in 2007, three in four of all new heterosexual cases of HIV in Britain were among African immigrants and on current trends by 2010 there will be more than 50,000 new HIV patients needing treatment in London alone, each costing the taxpayer up to £181,000 per person. The vast majority of these people contracted the HIV virus from overseas before moving to Britain, says the Health Protection Agency. None was tested before entering the county.

It is estimated that the average lifetime treatment cost for an HIV-positive person is between £135,000 and £181,000. From 1998 to 2002 in the UK there were 7,706 diagnoses of HIV thought to have been heterosexually acquired in Africa. The Department of Health reported in 2001 that the estimated cost of treating this one particular group between 1998 and 2002 would be between £1.04 billion and £1.39 billion. No one even hazards a guess at the total bill for AIDS treatment as a factor of immigration and asylum up to the present day.

Foreign immigrants are still arriving in Britain at the rate of half a million a year. To remove one failed asylum seeker costs the taxpayer approximately

£11,000. Factor the cost of treatment for immigrant AIDS for instance or the added costs in more than 300 of our primary schools where more than 70 per cent of children don't speak English as a first language (that's nearly half a million children) and it's more than likely that even an electorate as tolerant as Britain's will demand that their representatives take drastic action when the inevitable rationing of resources deprives their families of food and shelter: demanding not only British jobs for British workers but British healthcare for British citizens as a right.

Take this situation and add to it a prolonged period of freezing temperatures, food and water shortages. England is twice as crowded as Germany, four times that of France and twelve times the US. How could Britain cope with such numbers in a climate-induced crisis? The straight answer is, it couldn't.

Jonathan Porritt, a patron of the Optimum Population Trust (OPT) and adviser to Gordon Brown on green issues, has advocated that the population of Britain needs to be reduced from its current level of 62 million to 30 million if we are to be able to live in a sustainable society. That's less people than there were around when Queen Victoria was on the throne.

Porritt has impeccable green credentials, but

despairs at the lack of urgency in dealing with the issue of over-population in Britain. He says:

> One thing that's always worried me about the environmental movement for the last 30 years is the environmentalists' inability to get their heads around the importance of population. I find it staggering that that is still downgraded as an issue. There's a sense it's somehow politically incorrect to talk about population. But the issue of population lies absolutely at the heart of the destruction of the natural world today. If we had to find a way of creating a sustainable future for a billion people, I can assure you it would be a great deal simpler and a lot better for the natural world than trying to find a solution for 6 billion people, let alone 9 billion. So ignoring population strikes me as being the biggest own-goal that the environment movement has ever scored against itself, and it really concerns me that that has meant politicians can get away with paying zero attention to probably the most important issue of our time.' (4)

The bad news is that, by the time the coming cold period reaches its peak in 2030, there will be 71 million people in Britain, 10 million more than today.

Should our civilisation survive the 30 terrible winters to come, Britain still has the problem of more people living abroad than almost any other country in the world, exiles who may well wish to return home when things turn nasty over there.

More than 198,000 British nationals moved overseas in 2005, bringing the total number of Brits abroad to more than 5.5 million. (2) An Institute for Public Policy report shows that almost one in ten Britons now lives abroad and that a British national emigrates every three minutes, predicting that another 1 million British nationals will move abroad over the next five years. When confronted by extreme heat waves, drought and hurricanes in the southern hemisphere, how many of the 1.3 million expats now living in Australia or the 760,000 living in Spain will want to come back? That's not even including those in the rest of Europe, New Zealand, India or the Caribbean. In 40 years time, Britain may be the best real estate in the world. As cool as Canada, with plenty of water, and a reduced population following three decades of freezing temperatures. All his, while the rest of the southern latitudes have endured huge temperature increases, drought and food shortages because of man-made global warming.

The free society we in Britain know today will, by then, have ceased to exist. We depend on imports for around 70 per cent of our food. Without the ability to grow or access adequate supplies of food, fresh water and heat the following scenario becomes likely. Here is how it might feel for those at the sharp end of new immigration controls come 2025:

The Terrorism Act of 2000 had allowed the government to designate areas where police could stop and search citizens at will. In 2013 all of London became a stop and search area with even law-abiding citizens being arrested at gunpoint, DNA-swabbed and criminalised without the need to prove reasonable cause or produce evidence. Every vehicle entering the City is monitored by CCTV cameras; those who look suspicious are arrested. By 2025 the United Britain Party is the party of government; Britain is effectively a police state with a mission to remove those without the 'right' to remain here and has an arsenal of new laws that empower the use of deadly force against those who threaten the state. The midnight Eurostar crawls into Moseley station, a transit stop on the way to Waterloo. On board the passengers look nervously at one another and then down the aisle at the conductor who calls out: 'All passengers have their identity documents and ration cards ready for inspection, please.'

Looking out the window at the brightly lit platform those without papers try to quell their mounting panic as they catch sight of the UK Border Force. One armed officer placed every 10 metres dressed all in black, black visors pulled down from white crash helmets, submachine guns lowered as the train approaches. Everywhere are huge signs, in English with Urdu and Arabic translation. HAVE YOUR PAPERS READY. ILLEGAL ALIENS WILL BE SHOT. Across the platform and ready to roll is the last train due to leave that night for the big detention centre near Calais. The huge container trucks are jam-packed with refugees and deportees, women, children, old and young, ready to begin their journey back to their place of origin. The noise is deafening: shouting, screaming, cries for help, babies in distress. All ignored by the armed guards standing ramrod straight and looking dead ahead.

The criteria for British citizenship have become increasingly stringent. Britain is no longer bound by the Human Rights Act which has been replaced by the British Nationality Act of 2020. All failed asylum seekers have been deported after having their assets sequestered by the courts to pay for the costs of transportation. All illegal immigrants and those granted temporary residence status have also been removed after lengthy stays in the Calais centre, jointly funded by the British and French governments. A points system has been introduced based on work *skills, community cohesion and legitimately accumulated assets to rate all members of non-Europeans resident since 1997. This includes Afro-Caribbeans, Africans, Indians and Asians. The rating system also assesses religious and political beliefs. It is believed that large numbers of Africans never tested for AIDS, Muslims who cannot speak English fluently and anyone granted citizenship since 1997 with a criminal record are destined to be forcibly removed by 2030. Opinion polls suggest that this course of government action meets with huge levels of public approval.*

That's fiction *at the moment* but don't be fooled by government assurances, we're a heartbeat away from this crisis. At this point, another banking collapse or a mutation of the Swine flu virus could usher in large-scale social unrest before the cold spell of 2020 to 2050 delivers a knock-out blow.

CHAPTER FOUR
THE POLITICS OF GLOBAL WARMING

Scientists are currently engaged in fighting internecine wars over various explanations of the global-warming trend. Unfortunately, with over $50 billion in research grants made up of mostly taxpayers' money at stake, political concerns may have crept into their equations.

In 1988, James Hansen, a respected NASA climatologist, told the US Congress that temperature would rise 0.3°C by the end of the century and that sea level would rise several feet.

In 1991, he correctly predicted that the eruption of Mount Pinatubo in the Philippines would put a halt to the warming trend he had observed since 1990, although he had to wait until the 20 megatons of heat-reflecting volcanic dust had settled. Pinatubo had lowered the average global temperature significantly and Hansen's computer modelling had called it correctly. In 1996, he announced that 1995 had been the hottest year ever worldwide with an average temperature of 15.3°C (59.7°F).

In response, the UN set up the IPCC, and British taxpayers met the entire cost of its scientific team which produced the Third Assessment Report in 2001. This was a huge document presenting the world with the now infamous hockey stick graph, a product of climatologist Michael Mann, then at the University of Virginia (*fig 2*). He had attempted to work out the average global temperature over the past millennium. As direct temperature measurements only go back as far as 1860, to look further back in time his team had to use proxy records of temperature, such as the annual rings of trees, isotopic ratios in corals, ice-core science and the examination of lake sediments.

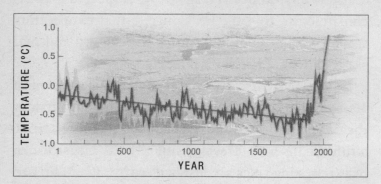

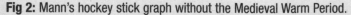

Fig 2: Mann's hockey stick graph without the Medieval Warm Period.

It was pioneering work and the first version of the hockey stick graph, showing average temperatures in the northern hemisphere going back to 1400, was published in *Nature* in 1998.

The next year, the team extended the reconstruction back to 1000, relying on the few proxy records that go back that far. This 1999 version appeared in the 2001 IPCC report.

The UN's second assessment report, produced in 1996, showed a 1,000-year graph demonstrating that temperature in the Middle Ages was warmer than today, the MWP became accepted fact.

The flat AD 1000–1900 temperature line was the shaft of the hockey stick and the up-line from 1900 to 2000 was the blade of the hockey stick. But in the IPCC's 2001 report the hockey stick graph showed no MWP and asserted that the 20th century was the warmest for 1,000 years. It turned out that there had been some errors and omissions. The proxy records had been assembled by researchers around the world, but their reliability was debatable and there were big regional differences. The graph gave too much weight to data which the UN's 1996 report had said was unsafe, namely the measurement of tree-rings from bristlecone pines. Tree-rings are wider in warmer years, but pine-rings are also wider when there's more carbon dioxide in the air. As Professor David Bellamy points out, CO_2 is plant food and this carbon dioxide fertilisation distorts the calculations. They said they had included 24 data sets going back to 1400 but had left out the set of data showing the MWP. The point being that, if it could be shown that a global increase in temperature is not necessarily the work of man but of a normal cyclical event, then the whole 'CO_2 causes global warming' theory looks much less convincing.

This is what the report said about the causes of climate change: 'Human activities are modifying the concentration of atmospheric constituents that absorb or scatter radiant energy. Most of the observed warming over the last 50 years is likely to have been due to the increase in greenhouse gas concentrations.' (1)

It was established that the concentration of carbon dioxide in the atmosphere had risen over the past 250 years to such an extent that CO_2 now constitutes almost 0.01 per cent more of the atmosphere than in the pre-industrial era. However, on the question of whether that alteration has had any detrimental climatic significance, there is no clear consensus. Many eminent scientists say that man-made greenhouse gases are warming the atmosphere, ice sheets are melting and the polar bears are in danger of extinction. Yet these assumptions can be easily contradicted by different sets of climate data. For instance, since 1894, the World Glacier Monitoring

Service based in Switzerland has built up a long and uninterrupted database on glacier changes. The group has observed that since 1980 there has been an advance of more than 55 per cent of the 625 mountain glaciers that they monitor across the world. They state that from 1926 to 1960 some 70–95 per cent of these glaciers were in retreat. The Antarctic, which holds 90 per cent of the world's ice and nearly all its 160,000 glaciers, has cooled and gained ice-mass in the past 30 years, reversing a 6,000-year melting trend.

Look closely at the CO_2 and temperature data and you find that increases in CO_2 are actually following increases in temperature and that CO_2 doesn't cause warming. On the contrary, warming causes CO_2 to increase. Ice-core samples had already shown conclusively that CO_2 rises *follow*, rather than *lead*, the Earth's temperature rise. CO_2 fluctuations actually follow the change in sea temperature, and, as any oceanographer will tell you, as water temperatures rise, oceans release additional dissolved CO_2.

World-renowned climatologist Wallace Broecker said that Mann's hockey stick could not be correct because it did not show the Little Ice Age or the MWP after AD 1000, which most tree-ring chronologies do show. His point was that tree-ring records alone won't be enough when it comes to measuring global temperatures because they are biased towards temperate North America and Europe. It was a point seized on by many sceptics.

'The hockey stick, the poster-child of the global warming community, turns out to be an artefact of poor mathematics,' said physicist Richard Muller. (2)

A House of Lords report in 2005 also commented on the IPCC process, and concluded:

We have some concerns about the objectivity of the IPCC process, with some of its emissions scenarios and summary documentation apparently influenced by political considerations. There are significant doubts about some aspects of the IPCC's emissions scenario exercise, in particular, the high emissions scenarios. The Government should press the IPCC to change their approach. There are some positive aspects to global warming and these appear to have been played down in the IPCC reports; the Government should press the IPCC to reflect in a more balanced way the costs and benefits of climate change. (3)

The hockey stick turned out to be the big attention-grabber in the 2001 report. It was shown six times and the Canadian government sent out a copy of it to every household in the country. Since then, dozens of scientific papers have shown that the MWP was real, with global temperatures up to 3°C (37.4°F) warmer *No!* than they are now. Then, there was very little ice at the North Pole. Historical records show that in 1421 a Chinese naval squadron sailed right round the Arctic and found none. It was also warmer in the Bronze Age and in Roman times when they grew grapes as far north as York. However, many other studies since Mann's have roughly confirmed his thesis about man-made warming over the last 25 years or so. He may have been wrong about the MWP but he was right about man's effect on climate. So why was it so balmy in Bronze Age Britain?

The most likely explanation is that it wasn't CO_2 that caused these warm periods, but the sun.

The sun's warming influence on the Earth is a two-step process. The first element of the warming equation is the action of the Earth's orbit around the sun. Due to gravitational planetary anomalies, the orbit of the Earth slowly changes over time, as does the orientation of the planet's spin axis. These changes induce variations of the solar radiation received on the Earth's surface that are responsible for some of the large climatic changes of the distant past.

Scottish scientist James Croll had developed a theory of the effects of variations of the Earth's orbit on climate cycles in 1875. He predicted multiple ice ages in 22,000-year cycles lasting 10,000 years each. The theory was flawed but revisited and revised by the Serbian mathematician Milankovitch in his theory of the paleoclimate in 1941. The succession of the ice ages that occurred during the Pleistocene epoch between 10,000 years and 1.8 million years ago was shown to be related to the periodic changes of the Earth's orbit.

Milankovitch found that the Earth wobbles in its orbit. This tilt is what causes seasons, and changes in the tilt of the Earth change the strength of the seasons. The seasons can also be accentuated or modified by the degree of roundness of the orbital path around the sun. Changes in the tilt of the earth can change the severity of the seasons: more tilt means warmer summers and colder winters, while less tilt means cooler summers and milder winters. The Earth wobbles in space so that its tilt changes by between 22 and 25 degrees on a cycle of about 41,000 years. Orbital changes occur over thousands of years, and the climate system may also take thousands of years to respond to orbital forcing. His theory suggests that the primary driver of ice ages is the total summer radiation received in northern latitude zones where major ice sheets have formed in the past, near 65°N.

Since then, the Milankovitch theory that the

variation of the Earth's orbital parameters regulates some of the major changes in the Earth's climate has been confirmed from other sources. In 1976, the landmark work of Hays, Imbrie and Shackleton (4) measured the change in continental ice volume over time by studying the isotopic ratio of oxygen in marine sediments. They found that the ice ages that occurred between 10,000 and 1.8 million years ago were related to the changes of the Earth's orbit and rotation.

Given that ice ages happen with a regular rhythm, it seems likely that cool temperatures will return at some point. Because we are about 10,000 years out from the last major ice age and if ice ages do recur every 10,000 years or so, it looks like our time in the sun may be almost up.

Core samples of ice taken from Russia's Vostok Station in Antarctica have produced evidence of Earth's atmosphere and temperature for the last 420,000 years. This evidence suggests that this 10,000 years of warmth we call the Holocene period is now almost over.

The problem with all this though is the extreme length of time taken for solar cycles to move around the sun, some 15,000 years for just one cycle. This is separate and different to the more observable 11-year cycle of sunspot activity.

The trouble is that mankind hasn't been around

long enough to know how long the sun goes without sunspot activity on a regular basis. We don't know because we don't have records going back millions of years, which is what we need to answer the question. What we do know is that sunspot activity has a direct relation to the weather on Earth. This is the second step of the sun's warming process and by far the most important to life on Earth.

Henrik Svensmark, a weather scientist at the Danish National Space Centre, has led a research team whose results show that the planet has been through a natural period of low cloud cover due to fewer cosmic rays entering the atmosphere. This, he says, is responsible for much of the global warming we are experiencing. He claims carbon dioxide emissions due to human activity are having a smaller impact on climate change than scientists think.

Svensmark thinks that the calculations used by the IPCC to make their predictions overlook the effect of cosmic rays on cloud cover and that the temperature rise due to human activity may be much smaller.

He said:

It was long thought that clouds were caused by climate change, but now we see that climate change is driven by clouds. This has not been taken into account in the models used to work out the effect carbon dioxide has had. We may see CO_2 is responsible for much less warming than we thought and if this is the case the predictions of warming due to human activity will need to be adjusted. (5)

We will look at this later on because for Britain the new sun cycle 24 will lead to freezing temperatures for the northern hemisphere for a generation to come.

The latest IPCC report adjusted its calculations to all but extinguish the sun's role in warming by dating its influence on temperature (or forcings) from 1750 when the sun, and consequently air temperature, was almost as warm as it is now. However, its starting date for the increase in world temperature was given as 1900, when the sun and temperature were much cooler.

The MWP is important here. The IPCC's charter presumes a widespread human influence on climate and, although its principles state that a wide range of views should be sought when selecting climate authors and contributors, this is not always adhered to. The 'climate deniers' suggest that many scientists have a vested interest in collaborating with current thinking regarding anthropogenic warming, and, indeed, much of their argument is based on the controversy surrounding the existence and importance of the MWP.

In 1995, David Deming, a geoscientist at the University of Oklahoma, wrote an article reconstructing 150 years of North American temperatures from borehole data.

He later wrote:

> With the publication of the article in *Science*, I gained significant credibility in the community of scientists working on climate change. They thought I was one of them, someone who would pervert science in the service of social and political causes. One of them let his guard down. A major person working in the area of climate change and global warming sent me an astonishing email that said: 'We have to get rid of the Medieval Warm Period.' (6)

The former US Vice-President Al Gore featured in *An Inconvenient Truth*, a film about climate change that was awarded the Best Documentary Oscar in 2007. Gore uses the hockey stick graph in the film and claims glaciers and polar bears are disappearing at an alarming rate, none of which turns out to be true. It didn't stop him winning the Nobel Peace Prize in 2007, either. Gore has since asked businessmen and investors to participate in the purchase of carbon offsets by investing in his company based in Britain, which buys stock in other companies.

An Inconvenient Truth focuses on the probability of a shutdown of the Great Atlantic Conveyor as predicted by the IPCC but concentrates on longer-term warming rather than short-term freezing, which it acknowledges is also likely. Al Gore, already a rich man, may get richer but the film still carries an important message about the need to adopt some form of eco-socialism if we are to avoid disaster beyond 2030.

As global temperatures have certainly risen by 0.4°C in the past 50 years, it seems reasonable to suppose that mankind may well have accounted for more than 0.2°C. There's still a debate about the actual figure. AccuWeather, a worldwide meteorological service, says that world temperature rose by only 0.45°C in the 20th century, while the US National Climatic Data Center says 0.5°C, and the UN believes it to be 0.6°C. If we allow for the impact of big polluting and fast-developing countries such as China and India, temperature may well rise by 0.6°C in this century. This is assuming that the record high levels of solar activity over the past 70 years do not decline. And there's the rub.

We know that we are putting large quantities of greenhouse gases into the atmosphere now and the consensus is that some warming has resulted; there is no real argument about that any more, and more warming will come as a result of greenhouse gases. What we still don't know is how much of the last 25 years' worth of warming of the planet is directly the result of man.

The Met Office Hadley Centre advises the UK government on climate change. Its work is jointly funded by the Department for Environment, Food and Rural Affairs (Defra), the Department for Energy and Climate Change (DECC) and the Ministry of Defence (MoD) and so is inextricably linked to government policy. In 2009, it ran 300 versions of their sophisticated climate computer model, and made broad predictions about climate change in the UK up until 2080. On 18 June 2009, the forecasts were released and warned that average mean temperatures are likely to rise by more than 2°C (35.6°F) across the UK by the 2040s and, if carbon emissions continue to rise, temperatures in the southeast could rise by 8°C (46.4°F) or more by the 2080s. These results are important because they are aimed at industry and other strategic planning organisations in the UK, and long-term investment decisions are taken as a consequence of these Met Office forecasts.

MPs have already passed the Climate Change Act 2008, committing the UK to restrict CO_2 emissions within 40 years to a level of less than 20 per cent of where they were in 1990. Short of closing down large sections of the economy, it is difficult to see where these cuts can be made, unless we say goodbye forever to economic growth, which may not be a bad thing but which leaves us with the thorny problem of a surplus population of 30 million or so by 2040. We could well be wasting billions of pounds planning for heat waves and droughts when what we need to be concerned with is the coming severe cold spell from 2020 to 2050. The Met Office seems to have got it very wrong, just like the 'barbecue summer' of 2009.

Here's another important point when it comes to devising national and global responses to climate change. The Met Office also maintains a global temperature record which is used in all of the reports of the IPCC. None of these forecasts takes any account of the role of the sun's influence. America, on the other hand, seems to have got it right with a much more pragmatic, wait-and-see approach. Before he was elected president, Barack Obama's stated goal was to reduce greenhouse-gas emissions to 1990 levels by 2020. Many scientists said that even this target fell short of the response needed.

NASA's James Hansen warned Obama that he may only have until 2012 to stabilise global CO_2 levels at 350ppm from current levels of around 380ppm to avoid the worst consequences of climate change. Given the levels of uncertainty here, one can sympathise with the new President's dilemma. He appointed a brilliant and outspoken 'warmer', Nobel Prize-winning physicist Steven Chu, as his new Energy Secretary, but Chu has already acknowledged that he won't be able to deliver the goods in time. In an interview with the BBC, he admitted that environmental targets will have to be watered down if legislation designed to cut US emissions is to be passed, that political factors would inevitably impact on US attempts to cut carbon emissions and that green groups should be prepared to compromise on emission targets in order to get climate-change legislation passed. (7)

Another eminent scientist, Dr Dennis Wheeler of Sunderland University, is firmly in the camp of those scientists who accept that man-made greenhouse gases are responsible for recent global warming.

Using the Climatological Database for the World's Oceans (CLIWOC), a scientific team led by Wheeler has examined more than 6,000 18th- and 19th-century logbooks from English, Dutch, French and Spanish fleets. His results suggest that Europe saw a spell of rapid warming during the 1730s, similar to that experienced today, resulting in changing weather patterns including increased frequency of storms.

The new research, compiled by Wheeler and colleagues from the Met Office and other institutions, is to be published in the journal *Climatic Change*. In an extensive interview with this author, Dr Wheeler expressed his fears about what man-made global warming could mean for Britain in the short term and for the rest of the world later on. This is a warmer's point of view:

GC: You mentioned your work with ship's logs and looking at weather patterns over time, you also mentioned the influence of the sun. There seems to be a fair amount of research, people like Sami Solanki, from the Max Planck Institute for Solar System Research in Germany, who say that declining solar activity could be a factor in the warming of the planet.

DW: This is where the message gets mixed. People look for single explanations and simple explanations why climate changes. All of the energy the atmosphere has is derived from the sun so it's fairly clear that if we get variations in the behaviour of the sun we are going to get variations in climate simply because of the difference in the energy inputs, but there are other factors at work as well. I mean there are oceanic circulation changes, there is continental drift, there's volcanic eruptions, there's also internal random variations and there's changes in the earth's orbit around the sun, which is small but we know are very important. So all of these things come into play, so if you look at the sun you've got to remember that it does vary but its output over the 11-year solar cycle is a fraction of 1 per cent, it's not much, and we know that, for example, in the late 17th century the sun was in a phase of relative quiescence. There were very, very few sunspots and the sun was much quieter than it is today and that's associated with the cold, certainly with the cold temperatures known as the Maunder minimum and it's certainly associated with the coldest years of the Little Ice Age, but once again we know that the Little Ice Age lasted longer than the period of the Maunder minimum so it doesn't give us the whole explanation.

GC: Certainly in terms of the IPCC reports it doesn't seem to be included to any great extent as a factor in global warming.

DW: It's not regarded as the controlling factor. I think there was a time, you know, before anthropogenic gases began to dominate the picture as they do at the moment, there was a time when you would look at volcanic eruptions, you'd look at solar influences, you'd look at changes in the Earth's orbit around the sun because they were the principle drivers to climatic variations, there was no question of that. But, if you look at what has changed since the Industrial Revolution, say since 1800, we're now in a wholly different climatic scenario, one in which the anthropogenic signal, for the first time one would argue, is beginning to dominate the picture. So it really, to some extent, doesn't quite matter what the sun does, its input, its variation has been swamped and taken over by anthropogenic factors. It's the first time in the history of the planet we've had this to deal with and certainly the CO_2, the methane, the nitrous oxide is rising at a rate which, you know, is unparalleled. Yes, if you go back through geological time hundreds of millions of years the composition of the Earth's atmosphere was different to how it is now, but it's been more or less stable, certainly for the last few million years, long before human beings came on the scene.

GC: Why is CO_2 bad for the planet?

DW: It's not bad for the plane, actually it's not bad at all because we have a natural greenhouse factor which operates anyway. For example, if we didn't have any greenhouse gases in our atmosphere, then the global temperature, average temperature would be plus 15 which it is, you know, between the North Pole and the equator. If we didn't have any greenhouse gases, it would be minus 18 and we could probably only live in a fairly narrow latitudinous zone around the equator.

GC: So what's the problem, why are we so worried about increasing CO_2?

DW: The problem is what's happening now as we put more and more CO_2 and related greenhouse gases into the atmosphere is actually inflating that greenhouse effect. Now, most life systems have adapted to the normal variations of greenhouse gases and so on and so forth, and if we have more greenhouse gases the temperatures are going to rise, you're going to get some pretty major climatic changes.

GC: Do you believe there is a link between CO_2 and temperature rise?

DW: Yes, well, there is, unquestionably, because it's a scientifically proven fact that we do have a greenhouse effect and that bizarrely is what makes life tolerable for us. What is going to make life intolerable is if we allow it to increase to such a level where we have major changes in the Earth's climatic system. Now, had this happened 10,000 years ago, you could argue it wouldn't have mattered. Human beings would have done what they have always done and they did until about 5,000 years ago. They would simply move; they would migrate from one part of the planetary system which it didn't like because it was getting too dry or too wet or too hot, you'd go somewhere else. We can't do that now; you see at first hand how difficult, migration, immigration, what a problem that is, we can't move any more. We've got political boundaries, we cannot make those political moves and our agricultural system is locked in to fairly narrow climatic margins, and, if you begin to interfere with the climatic system and that has impacts on agriculture, you've got serious problems of world food supplies.

GC: What I'm interested in is that you are firmly of the belief that this rise in CO_2, this warming is man-made.

DW: It's anthropogenically driven. There is no satisfactory explanation that offers any other means of accounting for it. Variations in the sun, but they are so trivial, they are so small, it's almost impossible to amplify that tiny signal into the kind of consequences that we have in terms of temperature changes that we see over the last 20 years or so, and they have been phenomenal.

GC: What about warm periods in the past when the planet has been as warm as it is now, say, during the Medieval Warm Period?

DW: Well, the Medieval Warm Period is questionable because, unlike today, some parts of the planet were warmer but there's clearly other parts of the planet which were not. There's difficulties in trying to detect the exact time of the Medieval Warm Period; it's different in some parts of the planet and different in others. You know, as the evidence accumulates, it becomes an increasingly patchy picture and people talk about, you know, vineyards in northern England and so on, but, you know, what changed vine production in Britain was, in part at least, change in economic conditions, competition with the French vine-growers; it doesn't hold together. Yes, it looks as if there was a period when some parts of Europe were warmer and there were periods when other parts of the world were colder. So the Medieval Warm Period which is often sort of offered as yeah, it was warmer in the past therefore there's no problem doesn't stand up to particularly close scrutiny as the evidence accumulates from around the world, and it takes a long time and a lot of money to gather this kind of evidence together.

GC: There's a school of thought that says that CO_2 isn't actually causing global warming, it's actually lagging temperature change. How do you react to that?

DW: If you look at the ice-core records, and we can go back about 800,000 years with the current Antarctic ice-core series, and it's unlikely we'll ever push it back much further than that, but there is certainly a suggestion there that temperatures were following changes – sorry, that CO_2 was following changes in temperature. And there are scientific reasons why it should do that like mildly to do with the change in temperature inside the atmosphere but the oceans which were big CO2 sinks, but once again we come back to the point that what we are now... it is a different game. We have interfered, inadvertently, with the climatic system and the old society with principles the same, but they're being expressed in a different way, and there's little doubt now that there's, you know, the temperatures and the CO_2 variations go very much in tandem. And on a scale, you know, rapidity which is pretty much unprecedented.

GC: There's another school of thought which says man's contribution to greenhouse gases is relatively insignificant, that water vapour is 95 per cent of the atmosphere and CO_2 isn't even a significant greenhouse gas.

DW: Well, it's the most significant of the greenhouse gases in terms of volume, in terms of its contribution to the atmosphere it's about 350 parts per million at the moment, which isn't very much, but it doesn't need to be much because of its effect. It doesn't matter that it's a trace element, I mean, if you look at methane and nitrous oxides are even more scarce in the atmosphere, even lower ppms for those. But the fact is that they are so uniquely responsive to outgoing long-wave terrestrial radiation, which oxygen and nitrogen are not. The main composition of the atmosphere is 99 per cent oxygen... to a greater or lesser extent they are inert. They don't respond directly to solar radiation coming in and they don't particularly respond directly to long-wave radiation going out. Greenhouse gases do but the fact that they are a small proportion of the atmosphere, a very small proportion, is really not of any significance in the argument whatsoever. The simple scientific fact is they behave the way they do on very, very sound scientific principles. We know they have this massive warming effect on the atmosphere.

GC: Just to get back to the debate about solar

science, it seems, looking at it from a layman's point of view, that the sun would be a huge component in warming the Earth, much more significant than man's contribution, especially when it comes to warming the oceans, I mean, it doesn't seem to feature in any of the major debates about the causes of ...

DW: Well it does, if you think about the variation from summer to winter across the latitudes due to effectively variations in solar energy receipts. It's colder in winter because the hours of daylight are shorter, warmer in summer because the hours of daylight are longer, and obviously that's well understood. But the variations that would account for the kind of global annual temperature changes that we see around us now just don't fit in with the absolutely trivial variations; we're looking at a point one of a per cent change in solar output between the solar maximum and the solar minimum on the 11-year cycle. And it just doesn't help us to explain the kind of temperature changes that we're getting now. It's got to be internal; it's got to be something that's changing within the Earth's very, very complex climatic system which has all sorts of feedback mechanisms which can divert energy from one partitioned area to another. If you've got more greenhouse gases, you're going to get more atmospheric heating, not because of the effect of incoming radiation but because of the effect of outgoing terrestrial radiation. Incoming solar radiation does not heat the atmosphere in any genuinely direct sense; what heats the atmosphere is the fact that the Earth's surface is heated, be it land, sea, forest, built-up area, whatever it is. That's heated, and that heat is communicated by conduction and convection to the atmosphere, but the Earth is also radiating and as that outgoing long-wave radiation, which is quite different to incoming short-wave radiation which the greenhouse gases kind of, if you like, tune into almost literally and convert that outgoing infra-red radiation to heat, and therefore the atmosphere becomes warmer.

GC: A lot of scientists have said, including Dr David Bellamy, that the more greenhouse gas the better, civilisation flourishes in a warmer climate, more food production...

DW: This is the point, you get one or two people making these arguments and they represent a tiny proportion of the scientific community. The simple fact is that I'm sorry, David Bellamy, we have moved on from the time when 5,000 years ago civilisation could develop in slightly warmer times than you find today. In those days, as I said earlier, if there was a climatic shift, it was easy: you moved, you emigrated, you went somewhere else. The world's population was a fraction of what it is today and it could grow enough food, there'd always be somewhere to grow enough food to keep you going. There's always enough land to graze your animals so you've got meat. There are six thousand million people on the planet now, we don't have any margin for variation. If the continental interiors, which is where a lot of the world's grain supply comes from, if they begin to dry up and the grain supply falls and the Chicago grain markets cannot any longer supply the international markets to supply India and other countries like this, so they cannot step in and buy their food, we have got some serious problems, we can't afford to just dismiss this 'Oh, well, it's all random variation and everything will sort itself out,' because, I'm sorry, it won't sort itself out and I think that in 20 or 30 years time, and I know it's over the political horizon and I know it's over the horizon for most people, certainly my age, but our children and our grandchildren will have to deal with some pretty substantial problems when it comes to food supply, when it comes to water supply, when it comes to resource exploitation and when it comes to environmental issues such as, you know, melting of the ice caps, rising sea levels and so on and so forth. It's going to happen. I think the question is the degree to which it's going to happen and the rapidity. Our concern is that, if you take some of the more extreme scenarios, it can happen in a big way and it can happen very quickly. Yes, there are other predictions which drop the temperature increases by a degree or two but in the long run it ain't gonna make any difference; someone is going to have to pick up the tab on this one. It won't be my generation, but someone is going to.

GC: Hasn't temperature been decreasing since 1998?

DW: I don't know where you got that from, the long-term trend is most definitely upwards and it's continuing. Yes, you're going to get, ooh, like the last winter, we've had a cold winter. So we've had a cold winter; no one has said that global warming is going to be constantly upwards, you're going to get fluctuations as climate does vary. The long-term trend on a decadal scale is most decidedly upwards, you've only got to look at the events, you know, of

2006, 2007, the summers we've had. Yes, they were wet, that's what attracted our attention; they were stormy but they were all above average temperatures as well, just because they were wet and stormy don't mean they're cold. So the temperature trend is still most definitely upwards. Yes, you're going to get the odd cold winter, yes, you're going to get the odd cold summer but those cold winters and cold summers are not going to be as cold as the cold winters and cold summers in the past. We have short memories, we don't recall these things.

GC: I recall as a child in the 1970s documentaries about the oncoming ice age.

DW: OK, I'll tell you what Stephen Schneider said about this and he's absolutely right because he's the guy who promoted this. He said, if you go to the doctors, he'll issue a diagnosis and he gives you that diagnosis, and you get some more evidence, you get a few checks and you find your first diagnosis was wrong. You'd be a damn fool to stand by that first diagnosis. If you get more evidence, you get more information; you get to see more, you realise it wasn't right at the time, then it changes. And what has happened in the last 20 years is that we've got direct physical, measurable evidence of global temperature increases. If you look at the temperature changes during the 1970s, the temperature increased in the first part of the 20th century, and only stabilised out rather bizarrely because of the effect of atmospheric pollution. Particular material in the atmosphere was shading out some of the sunlight and temperatures kind of stayed kind of static for a while and people such as Nigel Calder got a bit anxious about, you know, the ice going to advance and so on and so forth. But it was speculation, the temperatures didn't actually decrease in any statistically significant way. I'm old enough to remember the 1975 and 1976 droughts, and anyone who thought there was going to be a real advance in the ice with those two summers really was living in cloud cuckoo land and since then temperatures have just gone up and up. It's been, you know, unyieldingly so. Yes, that was the case but, I mean, if you look at all branches of science, the things we said 30 or 40 years ago we wouldn't say now. And, you know, science has moved on in the last 20 or 30 years and, probably, nowhere more so than with climate. The climatic system is unbelievably complicated; no one is pretending they've got all the answers, no one is pretending they've got a complete view of the future, no one is pretending that our predictions either politically, economically or climatically are absolutely right but the evidence we have at the moment, and it's accumulated, is that temperatures are going to go up, are going to have a redistribution of rainfall. I'm not pretending there aren't other issues…problems of, you know, species depletion and of resource depletion irrespective of all of this but this is just added to the complex environmental issues that are coming; I don't want to separate it and, you know, offer it up as a wholly separate issue, because it isn't, we've got to see it within the wider context of how we manage the planet we live on because it is the only one we've got.

GC: A lot of the problems for the sceptics, or deniers as they're called, is they have a problem with this hockey stick graph that was presented initially by a guy called Mann.

DW: Mike Mann, yeah.

GC: And it's been used quite extensively in the IPCC's reports. There's an anomaly there that they totally discount the Medieval Warm Period.

DW: Yeah, the thing, the trouble with the hockey graph is it initially goes out, the point I made earlier with you. The Medieval Warm Period is a regional phenomenon. It wasn't global in the sense that the warming we have now today is genuinely and sincerely global, and so, if you take, as Mike Mann did, proxy records from around the world, then you're going to lose the regional signal of the Medieval Warm Period. In other words, it was not the global phenomenon that we have today.

GC: Shouldn't that have been presented as part of the hockey stick graph?

DW: If you want global temperatures, you get global temperatures and that's what he gave. If you want regional signals, he'll give you regional signals. If you want north-west Europe or if you want the British Isles, he can give you temperatures for the British Isles, and in some parts of north-west Europe you will get a Medieval Warm Period and in some parts of Europe you'll get the Little Ice Age, but because of, as I said earlier, the nature of the Medieval Warm Period, yes, it was warm in Britain at that time, but it wasn't warm in other parts of the world, so, if you're averaging the cold bits and the warm bits, it disappears. And what's worrying is, when you look at what's happening today, around the world, we ain't got any cold bits. Everything is getting warmer, and that's the point, that's the point if you look at it globally, you do have this big temperature... yes, we can go back to the Medieval Warm Period and we know that it was drier and warmer, and in Europe it's been suggested that the climatic deterioration of the early 14th century caused such a political and social dislocation that it held back the Renaissance for a hundred years. That's probably true but in other parts of the world that wasn't happening, so to suggest that the Medieval Warm Period is some kind of wonderful analogue to what we've got today and therefore 'Don't worry, lads, let's just carry on polluting the atmosphere, everything will take care of itself,' you're living in a fool's paradise, and it'll be all right for you because, you know, we're not going to be around to see the worst consequences of this, and it's very easy to be dismissive, but we need to be aware that there's a very, very serious risk of the kind of environmental change which, yeah, if you go back 12,000 years, large parts of the planet were covered in ice and now they're not so, you know, you might argue that it's a better climate, but I come back to the point that the planet has changed because there are so many of us now, how are we going to live, how are we going to survive when margins are so tight now on population. One or two bad summers and harvest failures and, you know, the problems are serious. Two thousand years ago, couple of bad harvests, well, you just move on, you find somewhere else.

GC: You mentioned Nigel Calder before. His studies, as well as longitudinal studies by Landscheidt and many Russian scientists, are all of the opinion that we're actually coming to the end of a solar cycle that's going to lead us to a period of extended cooling, possibly offset in the long run by global warming.

DW: You know what they mean by the long run, don't you? 15,000 years. That's the scale at which these cyclic variations operate, and we haven't got time to wait 15,000 years for the change in nature of the Earth's orbit around the sun to kick in and temperatures to start falling. We're talking about decades and not millennia, and there are people, they're a small but highly vocal community and you can't put too much credence on their arguments. I don't know what political axe they have to grind, many of these people do. You think of the coal, oil and gas lobby in the United States which has traditionally supported sceptical research not because of interest in the side of the argument at all, they

The big freeze of 2009/10 was Britain's coldest winter in almost 30 years.

Prof. Bryden found that melting ice was slowing down the Gulf Stream.

©Rex Features

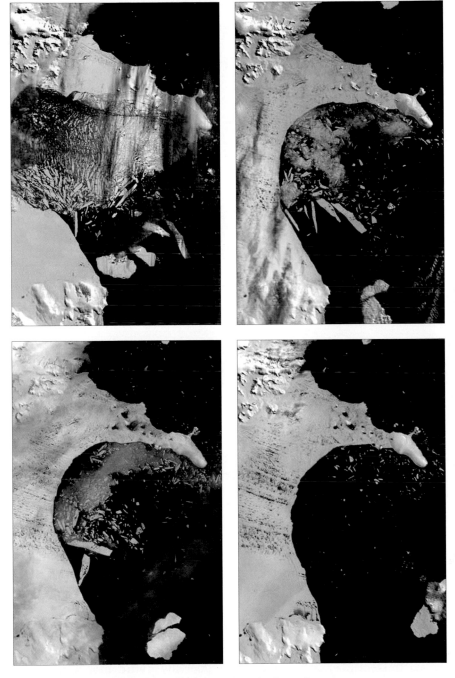

The Larsen B ice sheet breaks up and melts into the sea. ©*Rex Features*

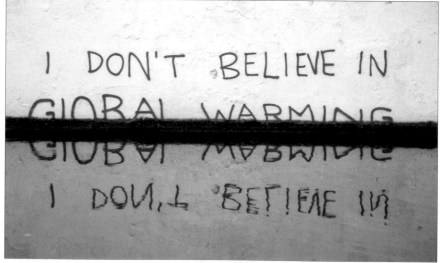

Above: Environmental activists protest at the 15th United Nations Climate Change Conference in Copenhagen, Denmark, December 2009.

Below: In December 2009, the infamous guerrilla graffiti artist 'Banksy' made his mark on a North London canal.

Above: Man-made global warming may be just a pinprick compared to the action of the sun.

Below: As the population grows and the climate changes food will be in increasingly short supply from 2020 onwards.

Above: There are huge oil and gas reserves on Sakhalin Island, Russia.

Below: Lovelock believes much of our planet will look like this by the end of the century.

The Amazon is being decimated to cater for the world's junk-food addiction.

Above: The Svalbard seed vault.

Below: NASA has plans to establish a moon base by 2050.

just want to make sure they sustain their sort of marketplace and that, you know, dirty fuel is not given a bad image. We all know what George Bush's view of this was.

GC: On a different tack, the work of Harry Bryden who is within your area of expertise. He says there could be a localised cooling in Western Europe and Britain because of glacial melt which would affect the system of... [Gulf Stream conveyance].

DW: There is not a shred of evidence... you show me anything which shows the temperatures have been decreasing in the British Isles. One of the very large number of scenarios that we have – this illustrates the point I was making earlier about regional climates – is that you do get melt water to the North Atlantic with the closure of the thermohaline circulation without the benefits of the Gulf Stream and temperatures over the British Isles could cool by 6 or 7 degrees (F), but the world ain't going to cool by 6 or 7 degrees, the world will carry on warming quite happily. But that's just one, it must be said, unlikely scenario.

GC: So it could be possible that within the larger context of global warming we could enter a period of localised cooling within our own... [backyard].

DW: Oh yeah, it's perfectly possible, it's what I said earlier about the Medieval Warm Period, it wasn't global and this wouldn't be global either. It would be highly localised, the coast of Norway, the British Isles, French coast and so on, without the benefits of the Gulf Stream.

GC: It wouldn't necessarily take a shutdown of the THC to cause that; it could just be a factor of the slowing of it.

DW: No, I mean, these circulation changes normally take, it's about 20 or 30 years for them to kick in and they do cause temperature variations that we've known about for some time. A couple of major episodes at the end of the Little Ice Age, at the end of the major ice age, for example the older Younger Dryas period, we know about those, but, yes, it could happen, but there's absolutely no suggestion whether it's going to, and a lot of those events constituted the melting of the Lawrentide ice sheet; well, the Lawrentide ice sheet has gone, all we're left with is the Greenland one, and the Lawrentide ice sheet was big but shallow and was subject to rapid changes and rapid thawing which could release large amounts of water. The Greenland ice sheet is just that, a little bit more inert to that one, so it may not behave in exactly the same way. Once again, we're in a different game now; the climate scenario's moved on from 10,000 years ago with the Younger Dryas which was associated with one of its effects, so we know from the deep-sea sediment cores in the North Atlantic that there have been episodes of ice coming out of the icebergs melting, the cold freshwater's been masking over the surface of the North Atlantic and it's caused a shutdown of the thermohaline circulation. Yes, it's happened in the past, it could happen in the future, but it's going to be purely regional in its extent; it's not going to change the temperature of the planet.

GC: So, basically, we could get an extended period of cold winters while the rest of the world is warming up.

DW: It's certainly possible, and that wouldn't be any better than warming for us. We would take even less satisfaction from that than from global warming.

GC: Because food production and ...

DW: Think of particularly, you know, hill farmers, marginal farming in Britain in Scotland for example, we know what happened in the Little Ice Age. Severe problems with crop failure in the late 17th century, all sorts of political and social problems resulting from that. It is not the kind of thing that you would want to repeat. (8)

CHAPTER FIVE
ALWAYS THE SUN?

Some of the first ever telescopic observations of our nearest star were made by Galileo in 1611. One of the first things he noticed was the presence of dark blemishes on the sun's surface, sunspots. Sunspots are regions on the solar surface where the energy supply from the solar interior is reduced because of strong magnetic fields. As a consequence, sunspots are cooler by about 1,500°C and appear dark in comparison to their non-magnetic surroundings which burn at a much hotter average temperature.

Thanks to Galileo and others who came after him, we know now that the number of sunspots rises and falls in approximately 11-year cycles. And the incidence of sunspots is important.

Two centuries ago, the astronomer William Herschel was reading Adam Smith's *Wealth of*

Nations, and he noticed that the price of grain always seemed to fall when the number of sunspots rose. Most thought this conclusion to be riotously funny, but it turned out he was right.

When the sun was at its hottest, more sunspots showed up and the temperature on Earth always seemed to be warmer, making grain grow faster and causing prices to fall because of the resulting glut. So, he concluded, more sunspots deliver more energy to the atmosphere so that global temperatures rise. Herschel's observations showed that even small changes in solar activity could affect our climate.

Although sunspots were first seen through a telescope in 1611, it was not until 1843 that an amateur German astronomer, Heinrich Schwab, specifically noticed and recorded the periodic rise and fall in their numbers. He observed the sun from Dessau, Germany from 1826 to 1868, and Schwab's yearly spot counts provided a means of describing the features of the sunspot cycle and the timing and relative strengths of each cycle, its minimum and maximum.

This became known as the Schwab cycle, which is made up of alternating five-and-a-half-year periods of high and low sunspot activity, an 11-year cycle. Up until Schwab's detailed records, there had been a curious absence of sunspot recording for the years between roughly 1611 and 1843, so much so that it took many years for modern astronomers to catch up with the missing data. That is, until the explanation for the gap in sunspot observation over that period of time became obvious, a nearly complete absence of sunspots for 70 of those years, roughly between 1645 and 1715.

For reasons not yet understood, the solar cycle was greatly reduced during that time. Evidence suggests it did not disappear entirely, but that the sunspot number, an index representing the total level of sunspots at any given time, was markedly reduced.

This strangely low sunspot record was detected by the astronomers F.W.G. Sporer and E.H. Maunder in 1890, and became known as the Maunder minimum, the name now given to this period of extreme solar inactivity (*fig 3*).

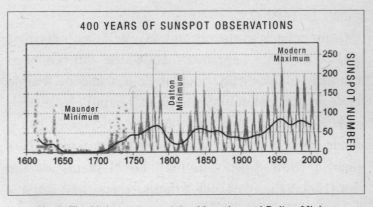

Fig 3: The Little Ice Ages of the Maunder and Dalton Minima coincided with low sunspot activity.

Why this is important is because the Maunder minimum period corresponds almost exactly with the Little Ice Age in Europe.

The existence of this Maunder minimum suggests that the regular rise and fall of sunspots, observed from 1715 all the way through to the present day, may not be a permanent aspect of solar behaviour.

The Spörer minimum of 1400–1510 and the Maunder minimum of 1645–1715 each corresponded to a Little Ice Age on Earth. They were both marked by an absence of sunspot activity, and link to abnormally cold weather on our planet.

The historical data show us that, in addition to finishing off the Greenland colonies, the Spörer minimum preceded increased rates of famine in Europe and that the Baltic Sea froze solid in the winter of 1422–23.

Coming back to the present day, what is interesting is that, as of 27 September 2008, the sun has been strangely blank again. That is, it has had no visible sunspots for 200 days of the year. To find a year with more blank suns, you would have to go back to 1954, when the sun was blank 241 times. What we have gleaned from direct satellite measurements of the sun's radiant activity shows that more sunspot activity from the sun delivers more energy to the atmosphere, so global temperatures should rise. Lower-than-normal temperatures occur in years when the sunspot cycle is longest, as confirmed by records of the annual duration of sea ice around Iceland. The cycle will be longest again in the early 2020s. That's when winters in Britain will come back with a vengeance, and may stay at arctic strength until 2040.

Even the standard 11-year cycle seems to have different strengths, with some of them showing more sunspot activity than others. The strengths of the cycle peaks seem to follow a roughly 80-year period of very strong cycles, slightly weaker ones, then back to stronger ones.

Examinations of the solar activity cycle and the unusually cold weather of the Maunder minimum period have caused great controversy among astronomers and climatologists. What we do know is that the Little Ice Age in Europe was characterised by unusually long and cold winters. This period coincides almost exactly with the period of time during which the sun is known to have been inactive, with some of the worst weather occurring bang in the middle of the Maunder minimum, when frost fairs were held on the frozen-solid River Thames.

Studies concerning the origin of solar activity and its effect on Earth's climate since 1610 needed to be much more detailed to make accurate predictions. In 1991, two Danish meteorologists published a paper pointing out a remarkably strong connection between the length of the solar cycle and global temperatures in the northern hemisphere. They found that not all cycles are the same 11 years in length. Longer cycles of 12–14 years tended to indicate cooler global temperatures than the shorter nine- to ten-year cycles. (1)

It is very difficult to assess the effect of even recent solar cycles on global climate let alone those from the Maunder minimum period because of the relatively short time span for which detailed observations exist, and because climate records are so rare and unreliable if you go back more than a century or so. However, there is no doubt the Maunder minimum years were a time of significant misery in Europe with long, harsh winters leading to shortened growing seasons, failed crops and widespread famine. Whether, or to what degree, the sun is responsible for this is an important question.

A couple of climate-change sceptics who believe the dangers of global warming are overstated have bet $10,000 that the planet will cool over the next decade. Russian solar scientists Galina Mashnich and Vladimir Bashkirtsev have agreed the bet with British climate expert James Annan. The pair, based at Irkutsk, at the Institute of Solar-Terrestrial Physics, believe that global temperatures are driven more by changes in the sun's activity than by greenhouse gases. They say the Earth warms and cools in response to changes in the number and size of sunspots and as the sun is expected to enter a less active phase over the next few decades they are confident that there will be a big drop in global temperatures. (2)

The scientific literature shows that in the last 2 million years the Earth has been subject to approximately 17 Ice Ages. It seems ridiculous to assume that these periods of major climate and temperature change have now suddenly stopped altogether. And what of the future, will we freeze or fry?

This is the conclusion of members of the National Academy of Sciences, a non-profit US organisation providing a public service by working outside the framework of government to ensure independent advice on matters of science, technology and medicine. The Academy enlists committees of leading scientists, engineers and other experts to advise on policy. All of these experts volunteer their time to study specific concerns. These were their conclusions:

The evidence of periods of several centuries of cooler climates worldwide called little ice ages, similar to the period anno Domini (A.D.) 1280–1860 and reoccurring approximately every 1,300 years corresponds well with fluctuations in

GAVIN COOKE

modelled solar output. A more detailed
examination of the climate sensitive history of
the last 1,000 years further supports the model.
Extrapolation of the model into the future
suggests a gradual cooling during the next few
centuries with intermittent minor warm-ups and
a return to near little-ice-age conditions within
the next 500 years. (3)

The sun is now going through a severe down trend in
sunspot activity and we are likely to soon find
ourselves back in a state similar to the Maunder
minimum with decades of much colder weather. Why?
Because, for most of recorded history, planet Earth
has been in the grip of various ice ages. This is
possibly because the sun doesn't put out enough heat
to keep the Earth warm enough.

In March 2008, solar scientist David Archibald
presented the evidence he had gathered about the
upcoming solar cycle 24. This was the crux of his
argument. Archibald stated:

The evidence from the Hanover solar cycle length
to temperature relationship, and that of the other
cities in this presentation, is incontrovertible.
There will be a significant cooling very soon. Our
generation has known a warm, giving sun, but

the next generation will suffer a sun that is less giving, and the Earth will be less fruitful. The big consequence of this is that it will shrink the growing season. The 2.2 (°C) degree decline I am predicting will take two weeks off the growing season at both ends. Next decade will not be a good time to be a Canadian wheat farmer. For farmers further south, farm production will decline but that production will be worth a considerable amount more. (4)

NASA solar physicist David Hathaway has studied international sunspot counts stretching all the way back to 1749 and offers these statistics:

The average period of a solar cycle is 131 months with a standard deviation of 14 months. Decaying solar cycle 23 (the one we are experiencing now) has so far lasted 142 months, well within the first standard deviation and thus not at all abnormal. The last available 13-month smoothed sunspot number was 5.70. This is bigger than 12 of the last 23 solar minimum values. The surprising result of these long-range predictions is a rapid decline in solar activity, starting with cycle 24. If this trend continues, we may see the sun heading towards a Maunder type of solar activity minimum, an extensive period of reduced levels of solar activity. (5)

Solar cycles usually take a few years to build from solar minimum at the start of the solar cycle (the next one is 24 but at the time of writing had yet to officially begin) to solar max, which is expected in 2012. What is not in doubt is that this is the quietest sun we have seen for more than 100 years.

The activity of the sun over the last 11,400 years back to the end of the last ice age has been reconstructed by an international group of researchers led by Sami K. Solanki, a solar physicist, from the Max Planck Institute for Solar System Research. This team of scientists from Germany, Finland and Switzerland analysed the radioactive isotopes in trees that lived thousands of years ago. These were its conclusions. (6)

Solanki says that in the past half-century the sun has been warmer for longer than at any time in at least the past 11,400 years, contributing a base forcing (an extra amount of warmth) equivalent to a quarter of the past century's warming. His team found that you would need to go back over 8,000 years in order to find a time when the sun was, on average, as active as in the last 60 years. Based on a statistical study of earlier periods of increased solar activity, the researchers predict that the current level of high solar activity will probably only last for, at best, a couple of more decades.

In 2003, the research team had already found evidence that the sun is more active now than in the previous 1,000 years. (7) A new data set had allowed them to extend the length of the studied period of time to 11,400 years, so that the whole length of time since the last ice age could be covered. This study showed that the current episode of high solar activity since approximately 1940 is unique within the last 8,000 years. (8)

This means that the sun has produced more sunspots, but also more flares and eruptions, which eject huge gas clouds into space, than ever in the past. The origin and energy source of all these phenomena is the sun's magnetic field. It could well be that man-made global warming has just happened to coincide with the sun's largest burst of activity in the last 8,000 years and what we blame on man is really a sideshow, a pinprick of energy masking its true cause, the sun.

In order to look at solar activity even further back in time, Solanki's team needed data from other areas. This they found in the form of cosmogenic isotopes, radioactive nuclei resulting from collisions of cosmic ray particles with air molecules in the upper atmosphere. One of these isotopes is C-14, radioactive carbon with a half life of 5,730 years, and use of this C-14 isotope was already well known as being a method to determine the age of wooden objects. The measurable amount of C-14 produced in the atmosphere depends strongly on the number of cosmic ray particles that reach it. This number, in turn, depends on the level of solar activity characterised by sunspots.

During times of high activity, the solar magnetic field around the Earth provides an effective shield against these charged particles. Conversely, the intensity of the cosmic rays increases when the activity is low. So, higher solar activity leads to a lower production rate of C-14, and vice versa.

By a mixing process in our atmosphere, the C-14 produced by cosmic rays reaches the biosphere and becomes part of the biomass of trees. Some tree trunks can be dug up from below the ground thousands of years after their death and the C-14 stored in their tree-rings can be measured. In this way, scientists were able to assess the production rate of C-14 backwards in time over 11,400 years, right up to the end of the last ice age. The research group then used this data to calculate the variation of the number of sunspots over these past 11,400 years.

The researchers around Solanki stress that solar activity has been high since about 1980, while the global temperature has experienced a strong increase during that time. He doubts that the sun is the direct cause of the recent global increase in temperatures since 1980, but does not deny that short-term freezing in Britain and Western Europe is a distinct possibility.

His team predicts that, by 2020, the sun will be starting its weakest solar cycle of the past two centuries and this is likely to lead to unusually cool conditions on Earth. It is also predicted that this cool period will go on much longer than the normal 11-year cycle, as the Little Ice Age did, even though it has been discovered that the sun is brighter now than any time in the past 8,000 years.

As Solanki admitted, the increase in solar output was not enough to cause all of the past century's warming. Man has played his part in that, but there was another not fully recognised, yet vital factor at play.

In 2002, scientific papers from Veizer, Shaviv and Carslaw from the Danish National Space Agency may have found the missing link to the increased warming. They collectively demonstrated that, as the output of the sun changes, varying amounts of cosmic rays from deep space are able to enter our solar system. These cosmic rays enhance cloud formation, which, overall, has a cooling effect on the planet. They were able to show that the sun's solar wind, generated by sunspot activity, blows away deep-space cosmic rays. With fewer sunspots, there is less solar wind, more cosmic rays and more cloud formation. More cloud formation means more cooling of our planet.

In 2007, Henrik Svensmark along with Nigel Calder produced a fuller account of this theory in a book entitled *The Chilling Stars: A New Theory of Climate Change*. Their Cosmic Ray Theory says that cosmic rays make the clouds that form around Earth. Deep in space exploding supernovas continually spray the galaxy with cosmic rays, which consist of protons, alpha particles, electrons and heavy electrons. This mix of atomic bullets makes our low-level clouds. Svensmark's results show that the rays produce electrically charged particles and these particles attract water molecules from the air and cause them to clump together until they condense into clouds.

The wet clouds, thus formed, block sunlight and reflect its rays back into space, which has a cooling effect. In 2006, Svensmark and colleagues had been able to demonstrate experimentally how it's done, which involves adding sulphuric acid to condensed nuclei. Plankton, microscopic plants in the ocean, and to a much lesser extent volcanoes and fossil fuels continually restock the atmosphere with seeding specks.

The sun's magnetic field encloses its planets in a magnetic solar wind or heliosphere that shields us from many of the cosmic rays that exploding stars shoot our way. Sunspots, those dark spots made by pools of intense magnetism seen through a telescope, indicate heightened magnetic activity, which deflects more cosmic rays away from Earth. During the 20th century, the sun's magnetic shield more than doubled, and the sun had a lot of sunspots. Fewer cosmic rays reached Earth to make clouds, and global temperatures rose. When the sun's magnetic activity is weak and sunspots disappear, more cosmic rays hit the Earth's atmosphere to make clouds and we cool. Svensmark's theory of climate change adds credence to observations made over the last 400 years, since the advent of the telescope, that correlate sunspots with global warming and cooling. The number of cosmic rays hitting the Earth changes with the magnetic activity around the sun. During high periods of activity, fewer cosmic rays hit the Earth and so there are less clouds formed, resulting in warming. Low activity causes more clouds and cools the Earth.

He says:

Evidence from ice cores show this happening long into the past. We have the highest solar activity we have had in at least 1,000 years. Humans are having an effect on climate change, but by not including the cosmic ray effect in models it means the results are inaccurate. The size of man's impact may be much smaller and so the man-made change is happening slower than predicted. (9)

Most computer models suggest that of the 0.5°C (32.9° F) increase in global average temperatures over the past 30 years only around 10–20 per cent of the temperature variations were because of the sun. Others believe it may be as high as 50 per cent.

No!

Dr George Kukla of the Czechoslovakian Academy of Sciences is a pioneer in the field of astronomical forcing. He says that global warming always precedes an ice age. Each lasts about 100,000 years, punctuated by briefer, warmer periods called interglacials. We are in an interglacial now. This ongoing cycle closely matches cyclical variations in Earth's orbit around the sun.

Kukla says, 'The relationship is just too clear and consistent to allow reasonable doubt. It's either that, or climate drives orbit, and that just doesn't make sense.' (10)

There will be a big temperature change at some point but no one knows when this 'crash' into cooler temperatures will occur, although scientists expect it soon. This is mainly because the sun's polar field is now at its weakest since measurements began in the 1950s. A deep crash last occurred in the 17th century

– and that crash was the Little Ice Age, or the Maunder minimum.

To summarise, solar magnetic activity manifests itself in sunspots, flares and coronal mass ejections, which give rise to magnetic storms on Earth. For the past 50 years, solar activity has been abnormally high, but such grand maxima do not last forever. The current boom will inevitably be followed by a slump, although it is impossible to forecast exactly when this will happen, or how deep the ensuing slump or grand minimum will be (*fig 3*).

What is clear is that throughout the 20th century the sun was incredibly strong and active. This activity peaked in the 1950s and the late 1980s. The evidence shows that the sun became increasingly active at the same time as the Earth warmed. Yet, according to the current scientific consensus, the sun has only a minor effect on climate change.

Dean Pensell, of NASA, says, 'Since the Space Age began in the 1950s, solar activity has been generally high. Five of the ten most intense solar cycles on record have occurred in the last 50 years.'

Professor Nigel Weiss, Emeritus Professor in Mathematical Astrophysics at the University of Cambridge and 2007 winner of the Royal Astronomical Society (RAS) Gold medal, says, 'Having a "crash" would certainly allow us to pin down the sun's true level of influence on the Earth's climate. Then we will be able to act on fact, rather than from fear.' (11)

A declining trend in solar activity and global temperature is becoming clear in the latest sunspot cycle. The current 11-year sunspot cycle 23 with its considerably weaker activity is about to come to an end and seems to be a first indication of the new trend, especially as it was predicted on the basis of solar-motion cycles two decades ago by Dr Theodor Landscheidt. Landscheidt, who died in 2004, was the founder of the Schroeter Institute for Research in Cycles of Solar Activity in Waldmuenchen, Germany. He was the foremost authority on the workings of the sun and he said we should heed this warning:

Analysis of the sun's activity in the last two millennia indicates that, contrary to the IPCC's speculation about man-made global warming, that we could be headed into a Maunder minimum type of climate (a Little Ice Age). The probability is high that the minima around 2030 and 2201 will go along with periods of cold climate comparable to the nadir of the Little Ice Age... the current 11-year sunspot cycle 23 with its considerably weaker activity seems to be a first indication of the new trend, especially as it was predicted on the basis of solar motion cycles two decades ago. As to temperature, only El Niño periods should interrupt the downward trend, but even El Niños should become less frequent and strong. The total magnetic flux leaving the sun has risen by a factor of 2.3 since 1901 while global temperature on Earth increased by about 0.6°C. Energetic flares increased the sun's ultraviolet radiation by at least 16 per cent. There is a clear connection between solar eruptions and a strong rise in temperature. I [Landscheidt] have shown for decades that the sun's varying activity is linked to cycles in its irregular oscillation about the centre of mass of the solar system (the solar retrograde cycle). As these cycles are connected with climate phenomena and can be computed for centuries, they offer a means to forecast phases of cool and warm climate. Researchers need to take the sun seriously as a factor in climate change, including warming, droughts, and cold snaps. (12)

These results and many earlier ones (Landscheidt, 1981–2001) document the importance of the sun's activity on climate. Landscheidt had shown for decades that the sun's varying activity is linked to cycles, and these cycles are connected with the climate on Earth. They offer a means to forecast phases of cool and warm climate. Landscheidt's forecasts were usually correct and included the end of the great Sahelian drought, the last three El Niños and the course of the last La Niña. He also predicted the extreme River Po discharges beginning in October 2000 some seven months before they began, all based on solar activity. (13)

This forecast skill, says Landscheidt, solely based on solar cycles is at odds with the IPCC's assertion that it is unlikely that natural forcings, namely the action of the sun, can explain warming in the latter half of the 20th century. Landscheidt has a considerable body of research to support his claims. (14)

Landscheidt's analysis of the sun's activity in the last 200 years indicates that we are indeed headed into a new Little Ice Age. If we look at the evidence presented by scientists who believe the sun is a major influence on climate and weather patterns, the probability is high that his predicted minima around 2030 and 2201 will be similar to the periods of cold climate prevalent during the Little Ice Age. We don't need to wait until 2030 to see whether the forecast is correct, though. The odds are greater that we will have more years in the future with lower sunspot activity than with higher sunspot activity. Landscheidt states that: 'Analysis of the sun's varying activity in the last two millennia indicates that contrary to the IPCC's speculation about man-made global warming as high as 5.8°C within the next 100 years, a long period of cool climate with its coldest phase around 2030 is to be expected.' (15)

A decrease could put large amounts of farmland out of production and would reduce the length of the growing season. The freezing over of rivers and seas along with snows and ice would interfere with transportation, certainly more than higher temperatures would. The climate threat to us all in the short term is from rapid cooling, especially in Canada. In the far northern limit of the world's agricultural production, it wouldn't take very much cold weather to destroy most of the wheat crop. Canada and America, the bread baskets of the world, would see their growing seasons shortened by four weeks, with incalculable consequences for the price of wheat, and world hunger.

A team of more than 60 scientists from around the world is preparing to conduct a large-scale experiment using a particle accelerator in Geneva, Switzerland, to replicate the effect of cosmic rays hitting the atmosphere. They hope this will prove whether this deep space radiation is responsible for changing cloud cover. If so, it could force climate scientists to re-evaluate their ideas about how global warming occurs. If Landscheidt is correct, it could mean that mankind has more time to reduce our effect on the climate but that inevitably the sun's quiet spell will have severe cooling consequences for us all.

CHAPTER SIX
THE FIGHT FOR FOOD

In 2008, a US report by the National Intelligence Council made a detailed set of assessments of global trends up to 2025. The study, 'A Transformed World', predicts increased international conflict over food, water, energy and other scarce resources. It predicted that international institutions, from the IMF to the UN, will become less effective, owing to the multiplicity of new global players. America will no longer fill the role of the world's policeman and tribal groups, religious organisations and organised criminal networks will be increasingly dominant. Among the more alarming conclusions in the global trends report is the assertion that a government in Eastern or Central Europe 'could effectively be taken over and run by organized crime'. The report also speculates that some states in Africa or South Asia could disintegrate as their governments fail to provide basic services such as food, fresh water or healthcare to their populations.

This report does not take into account a world thrown into turmoil by drought, floods and freezing temperatures, cities like Amsterdam potentially submerged and other low-lying countries made uninhabitable.

The very near future may well look like this: the borders of the US and Australia patrolled by armed militia while at sea naval gunships fire live rounds into waves of starving people desperate to find a new home; fishing boats in Spain and Portugal armed with live ammunition to drive off competitors; desperate demands for access to water and farmland backed up with nuclear weapons in places like Pakistan and India.

In 2003, another report suggested that, because of the potentially dire consequences of abrupt climate change, our concerns should be elevated beyond a scientific debate to a full-blown national security concern.

The authors of this report warned:

There is substantial evidence to indicate that significant global warming will occur during the 21st century. Because changes have been gradual so far, and are projected to be similarly gradual in the future, the effects of global warming have the potential to be manageable for most nations. Recent research, however, suggests that there is a possibility that this gradual global warming could lead to a relatively abrupt slowing of the ocean's thermohaline conveyor, which could lead to harsher winter weather conditions, sharply reduced soil moisture, and more intense winds in certain regions that currently provide a significant fraction of the world's food production. (1)

There are strong indications that global warming has reached the threshold where the THC is already being significantly impacted. These indications include observations that the North Atlantic is now being freshened by melting glaciers, increased precipitation and fresh water runoff making it substantially less salty than over the past 40 years. With inadequate preparation, the result will be a significant drop in the human carrying capacity of the Earth's environment. The research suggested that temperature rises could result in abrupt changes in the atmospheric circulation that could last for as much as a century, as they did when the ocean conveyor collapsed 8,200 years ago.

A worst-case scenario is that a new ice age could last as long as 1,000 years, as happened during the Younger Dryas, which began about 12,700 years ago.

In this report, an abrupt climate-change scenario was outlined, patterned after a 100-year event that occurred 8,200 years ago. This abrupt change scenario is characterised by the following conditions: annual average temperatures drop by up to 5°F over Asia and North America and 6°F in northern Europe. Annual average temperatures increase by up to 4°F in key areas throughout Australia, South America and southern Africa. Drought persists for most of the decade in critical agricultural regions and in the water resource regions for major population centres in Europe and eastern North America. Winter storms and winds intensify, amplifying the impacts of the changes. Western Europe and the North Pacific experience enhanced winds.

The report explores how such an abrupt climate-change scenario could destabilise the geo-political environment, leading to skirmishes and even war due to food shortages, availability and quality of fresh water and disrupted access to energy supplies.

A reported probability of food shortages, even without severe climate change, came from the UN Food and Agriculture Organization (FAO) who warned the world on 17 December 2007 that reserves of cereals were dwindling fast. In that year, reserves of wheat had declined by 11 per cent, the lowest level since the UN began keeping records in 1980.

More than 100 countries now import wheat and 40 countries import rice. Egypt and Iran rely on imports for 40 per cent of their grain; Algeria Japan, South Korea and Taiwan import more than 70 per cent; and Israel imports more than 90 per cent. Just six countries – the US, Canada, France, Australia, Argentina and Thailand – supply 90 per cent of all grain exports. The US alone supplies grain to half the world.

Up to the year ending 2008, wheat exporters in the US sold off more than 90 per cent of what had previously been earmarked for export to world markets. This had terrible consequences for the developing world in particular, as their diets consist mostly of cereal grains imported from the United States. Agricultural researchers have predicted that in the central grain-growing area of the US there will be substantial reductions in the amount of moisture available to grow food by 2050. Many studies that assume the US can gear up its food production to meet the needs of larger populations don't take into account the lack of water available. In their 2001 report, the IPCC concluded that there were 1.7 billion people in the world without adequate supplies of clean water and that this figure was set to increase to some 5 billion by 2025.

According to the FAO, 37 nations currently face exceptional shortfalls in food production and supplies. Twenty of these countries are in Africa and two in Eastern Europe. Latin America and Asia are also at risk. Ironically, India, currently industrialising at a rate of knots, would be one of the most vulnerable nations to mass starvation. In India, traditional farming methods relying on human or animal labour have been replaced with the use of tractors and chemical fertilisers, and subsistence crops replaced by cash crops for exports or monocultures. It has been pointed out that traditionally Indian farmers burn about half a calorie in order to produce one calorie's worth of food. The new methods of farming use ten calories of non-renewable and polluting energy to produce the same one calorie.

More than 850 million people around the world suffer from chronic hunger and most of those affected live in countries dependent on imports. The very poorest, whose diets consist heavily of cereal grains, are most vulnerable. These are the poor who already spend up to 80 per cent of their income on staple foods.

Political unrest linked to food shortages has already taken place in Uzbekistan, Yemen, Guinea, Morocco, Mauritania and Senegal. In 2008, cereal prices sparked riots in several other countries, including Mexico, where tortilla prices rose by 60 per cent.

Many countries of the former Soviet Union are facing serious wheat shortages and in Bangladesh rice prices rose by 50 per cent in 2008. Central American countries also saw a 50 per cent increase in the price of the region's staples, grain and corn, that year.

All national governments are keenly aware of the possibility of civil unrest in the event of severe food shortages or famine, and many have taken steps to ease the crisis in the short term, such as reducing import tariffs and introducing export restrictions. On 20 December 2008, China did away with food-export rebates in an effort to stave off domestic shortfalls. Russia, Kazakhstan and Argentina also implemented food export controls.

Several countries in South America have also been impacted by the high international wheat prices, compelling national governments to dispense with import taxes. The government in Bolivia found it necessary at one point to send the army in to bake bread on an industrial scale.

On a macro-economic level, as the sub-prime housing market in the United States collapsed, problems in the credit market brought about recession. Speculators then shifted to the commodities markets, exacerbating inflation in basic goods and materials. The international food market is particularly prone to volatility because prices can be influenced by speculators. This speculation then triggers more volatility leading to more speculation.

Rice is a case in point. It is the staple diet of most countries in the Third World, and there isn't a lot of it. Only 8 per cent of the world's rice output is traded, so most rice-consuming countries have just about enough to survive.

Higher fuel costs also lead to higher food prices, via higher shipping charges, particularly for nations that import most of their staple foods. A rising oil price also has an impact on the costs of farming in the working of agricultural machinery and industrial processing.

As oil prices rise, demand for biofuel sources such as corn, sugarcane and soybeans also rises, resulting in more crops being devoted to fuel production.

Under the stewardship of George W. Bush, a third of the US corn harvest became converted to ethanol production, more than the amount of corn bound for all the world's food markets. This was because of perceived worries about US dependence on overseas oil. The use of corn for ethanol production has doubled since 2003, and is projected by the FAO to increase from 55 million tonnes to 110 million tonnes by 2016. This is how seemingly small decisions have massive consequences in our inter-connected world. The consequence of this particular policy was a world rice crisis in 2008.

As farmers in the US began to plant more corn in place of wheat to produce ethanol, the price of wheat began to rise on the world market. Higher wheat prices meant expensive wheat in Africa and Asia was replaced by the old staple of rice; faced with higher wheat prices, people began substituting rice in their diets, particularly so in Africa. The dominoes continued to fall, and India and Vietnam, the world's biggest rice exporters, saw the price of wheat and then rice go through the roof and in an attempt to keep a lid on domestic inflation announced export restrictions. For a time, there was no rice at all for sale on the world market. This led to the panic buying and hoarding of rice by traders. Over a period of 24 months, the price of rice rose by more than 200 per cent. There were widespread food riots in Egypt and Haiti, and the World Bank warned that more than 100 million people were now at risk of starvation.

On 19 December 2008, President Bush, in one of his last acts as chief executive, signed an energy bill into law which will expand US domestic biofuel production five-fold up to 2023 to more than 36 billion gallons a year. So, as more US cropland is given over to ethanol production to fill the tanks of gas-guzzlers, other major agricultural regions are struggling with weather disasters associated with climate change. Australia and the Ukraine, both big exporters of wheat, have suffered extreme weather that has severely damaged crops. A long drought in southern Australia throughout 2008 devastated farming to such an extent that many farmers called it a day and sold off their land.

Evidence from the Proceedings of the National Academy of Sciences of the United States of America suggests that as temperatures rise over the next 50 years by 1 to 2°C, (33.8 to 35.6°F) poor countries may lose 135 million hectares of arable land because of lost rainfall. In 2007 their study, Global Food Security under Climate Change, researchers cautioned that this estimate may be conservative and that the impact of climate change on food production has been oversimplified.

No!

As global and local carrying capacities are reduced, tensions will mount around the world, leading to two fundamental strategies: defensive and offensive. The strong nations with access to resources will build fortresses around their countries, preserving food, water and energy for themselves. Those with greater population pressures and a clash of beliefs, like India and Pakistan, will begin struggles for access to food and clean water, and, as they do so, they will see religion and ideology relegated as causes of conflict as nations struggle for survival.

CHAPTER SEVEN
POPULATION POSTULATION

How many people can the Earth support? This question has interested scientists for many years.

In his *Essay on Population*, published in 1789, 18th-century political economist and thinker Thomas Malthus explained the link between the growth in population and what he termed human 'misery and vice'. The essence of his argument was that unchecked population growth would eventually outstrip our ability to increase food production. Malthus argued that population always tended to push above the supply of food and so any attempt to improve the lot of the lower classes by increasing their incomes or living conditions would only serve to further increase the growth in population. Thus, Malthus became a hate figure for utopian and left-leaning thinkers of the 20th century who put their faith in a world without limits to growth or population, and opposed Malthus's claims that the working class were poor because there were too many of them, not because they were oppressed and exploited. He opposed welfare or higher wages because he believed that would allow the poor to breed, compounding overpopulation and leading to more poverty. A revised and expanded edition of his essay appeared in 1803 advocating that the working classes be encouraged to adopt middle-class values via state-funded education, universal suffrage and the abolition of the Poor Laws, so he may have had a bad press.

As it turned out, Malthus's theory was correct, but at the wrong time. There was no widespread famine and starvation as the population boomed from less than 2 billion in pre-industrial times to the 6.8 billion alive on our planet today.

What Malthus could never have envisaged was the surge in world food production that was to take place after his death with the coming of industrialised agriculture, powered by oil. As it happened, over the last 200 years, food production has actually grown faster than the population. Were it not for the anomaly of fossil fuels, his predictions would have been entirely accurate.

Others following in Malthus's footsteps have since

refined the argument on population with reference to environmental factors.

Carrying capacity is a term used by ecologists to describe the maximum number of animals of a given species that any given habitat can support indefinitely, without permanently degrading the environment.

In the 17th century, Dutch microbiologist Anton van Leeuwenhook estimated that the Earth could support a maximum of 13.4 billion people. A more scientific approach in the mid-19th century led German chemist Justus von Liebig to formulate his Law of the Minimum, based on the realisation that the addition of a single fertiliser will increase crop yield only if a particular soil can deliver all the necessary nutrients.

Using Liebig's law, we can say the population of humans, or any other species, will be constrained by whatever survival resource – food, water, heat, etc. – is in shortest supply. Using this approach, modern estimates for human carrying capacity have ranged from 1 or 2 billion people living in prosperity to 33 billion people fed on minimum rations and using all suitable land for high-intensity food production. Some scientists believe that the human carrying capacity of the Earth is approximately 12 billion, but that figure does not take account of global warming and climate change.

According to the UN (2010), the world's population is predicted to grow from currently 6.8 billion to 8.2 billion by 2030, with 1.2 billion in the developed and 7 billion in the developing world. But if the population of developing nations continues to grow at current levels the world will have 15 billion people by the end of the century. Worldwatch believes that increased scarcity of water will lead to world food shortage and this in turn will lead to future wars over water resources. There is already increasing tension between India and Pakistan over access to the Indus River, which Pakistan depends on to irrigate huge areas of land. Today, a billion people worldwide do not have access to clean supplies of drinking water.

On the other side of the world, the Mexican Water Treaty of 1944 made with the United States agreed to ensure that Mexico got 1.5 million acre-feet of water a year. However, for many decades, those south of the border often got more water than the treaty required if the flow on the river exceeded the water farmers north of the border could use. Mexico and its river ecosystem greatly benefited from the excess groundwater and water seepage draining from the All-American Canal, an 82-mile ditch that runs north of the border and diverts water from the Colorado River across the desert of southern California to farms in Mexico's Imperial Valley.

But a long drought in the southern states made the Colorado River authorities think twice about the arrangement and they instigated a plan to take more water out of the river. They decided to line 23 miles of the All-American Canal with concrete to prevent water seepage and also built a reservoir just north of the border to catch the excess flow going over the border. Water conservation from the project began in 2008, when two other segments of the project were completed, and the project's water-saving plan will be fully operational in 2010. The lining of the canal will then yield an extra 67,000 acre-feet of water a year and the reservoir another 60,000 acre-feet a year.

The project's water managers will no doubt declare they have stopped water wastage but the water that formerly seeped underground and flowed beneath the Mexicali Valley south of the border, feeding the fields of local farmers, will now be lost and have consequences for agricultural production in Mexico.

Victor Hermosillo, former mayor of Mexicali, declared before the canal was built: 'Encasing a new canal in concrete would divert more water for San Diego's emerging suburbs and golf courses, but it would do so with devastating impacts. By drying up the groundwater, the concrete canal would deprive many thousands of Mexicans of their livelihood, forcing them to migrate north. One expert predicts more than 30,000 Mexican jobs could be lost if the canal is built.' (1)

This is an example of how scarcity of resources can suddenly lead to hardship and potentially conflict.

In 2006, US farmers distorted the world market for cereals by growing 14 million tonnes of maize, or 20 per cent of its entire crop, for ethanol, to be used as an alternative to petrol in motor vehicles. This took millions of hectares of land out of food production and nearly doubled the price of maize. In 2007, President Bush called for further steep rises in ethanol production as part of plans for a 20 per cent reduction in demand for petrol by 2017. This followed an EU initiative of substituting 10 per cent of all car fuel with biofuels. Maize is a staple food in many countries including Japan, Egypt and Mexico which import it from the US. The US exports 70 per cent of the world total of maize, used widely for animal feed, and the shortages caused by these policies have severely disrupted livestock and poultry industries throughout the world.

The situation can only get worse as agro-industries switch from producing food to producing highly profitable, and subsidised, biofuels. The food crisis is being compounded by growing populations, extreme weather and ecological stress. Grain, a Barcelona-based food resources group, says that the Indian government is committed to planting 14 million hectares of land to produce bio-diesels, while Brazil intends to plant 120 million hectares for biofuels, and Africa as much as 400 million hectares in the next few years forcing millions of people off the land.

In 2007, the National Agricultural Marketing Council of South Africa reported that the country had become a net importer of agricultural products for the first time in more than 20 years as local food output failed to keep pace with a growing population.

That situation pales in comparison to what will happen in China, the world's most populous nation. As China industrialises, its population has increasingly shifted from the countryside to the big cities, like Beijing. Paddy fields that once grew rice and fed the nation have now been abandoned or used by industry to make cheap clothing for Western consumers. The result has been that, in 1995, China became a net food importer for the first time and the worldwide price of grain rocketed.

In 2008, the world was only ten weeks away from running out of wheat supplies altogether after stocks fell to their lowest level for 50 years.

China has experienced a fundamental change in its consumer habits. There and elsewhere in the Far East, growing wealth has been accompanied by a growing taste for Western junk food, most specifically for beef, which is now being imported by China in huge quantities. There was once a time when the very idea of a Big Mac meal would have made the average Chinese citizen retch, but not now. McDonald's have opened restaurants across China to cater for the appetites of a new generation and is now busy building a chain of drive-through fast-food outlets in China's 30,000 plus petrol stations.

The world market for beef, and the resulting need for cattle feed, has coincided with a decline in the production of grain, as the maize farmers of America switch from producing their standard crops to growing biofuels, as ordered by George W. Bush, lest America become too dependent on Saudi Arabia for its oil. Since then, Richard Branson, owner of Virgin Airlines says he intends to fly his planes across the Atlantic using biofuels. Should this crusade be taken up by other airlines, what would be the result?

World Bank analysts say that biofuel production has accounted for a 65 per cent rise in world food prices, while the IMF believes that biofuel production is responsible for a major jump in commodity prices.

China's growing industrialisation is also having a profound effect on wheat consumption. In his book *Who Will Feed China?*, Lester Brown says that if China continues its rapid industrialisation it will raise its total grain use from under 300 kilograms per person at present to 400 kilograms by 2030 (still only half the 800 kilograms per person consumed by those living in the US). He cited the consumption of beer as an example. In 1994 the Chinese were drinking 13 billion litres of beer, second only to the US. By 1998 this consumption had more than doubled. In 2006 a Business Insights report, Beer in China, revealed that share of volume beer sales (2001-2004) to China made it the world's largest consumer of beer. To raise beer consumption for each adult in China by just one bottle per year takes an additional 370,000 tonnes of grain. To supply three additional bottles per person would take the equivalent of Norway's annual grain harvest, says Brown.

China's growing grain consumption means it will need to import some 369 million tonnes of grain in 2030. Can China afford to import these massive quantities? You bet it can. In 1994, China's trade surplus with the US was nearly $30 billion, enough to buy all the grain from all the food-exporting countries. Can anyone supply China with this amount of grain? Definitely not. If China's rapid industrialisation continues, its import demand will soon overwhelm the export capacity of the US and other grain-exporting countries combined. But, in addition to China, more than 100 countries depend on the US for grain.

Brown states, 'With its grain imports climbing, China's rising grain prices are now becoming the world's rising grain prices. As the slack goes out of the world food economy, China's land scarcity will become everyone's land scarcity. As irrigation water losses force it to import more grain, its water scarcity will become the world's water scarcity.' (2)

In March 2008, Egypt decided to suspend rice exports for six months to meet domestic demand and to limit price increases. World rice prices soared by 30 per cent in one day and its main rice customers – Turkey, Lebanon, Syria and Jordan – were badly hit. This move prompted Vietnam, the world's second-largest rice exporter after Thailand, to cut rice exports by 25 per cent, and officials in Vietnam were told not to sign any more export contracts. India and Cambodia also moved to curb their exports in order to have enough supplies to feed their own people.

The bottom line is that, if China needs more than 300 million tonnes of grain yearly, then the rest of the world will starve, as this amount is more than the grain exports of all the grain-producing countries of the world.

'It's a perfect storm,' Professor John Beddington, the government's chief scientific adviser, told the Sustainable Development UK conference in March 2009. He warned the audience that a combination of growing populations and food, energy and water shortages will reach crisis point by 2030. 'My main concern is what will happen internationally, there will be food and water shortages,' he said.

Beddington predicted demand for food and energy will shoot up 50 per cent by 2030, while demand for fresh water will go up by 30 per cent. By then, the world population will have reached 8.3 billion, with climate change further destabilising the situation. According to the United States Census Bureau in February, 2010 there were slightly more than 6.8 billion people in the world, and this figure is growing by about 6.5 million people a month.

This is just too much for the carrying capacity of the planet, Beddington warned, 'If we don't address this, we can expect major destabilisation, an increase in rioting, and potentially significant problems with international migration, as people move out to avoid food and water shortages.' He added that he sees the year 2030 as the point at which things will start to fall apart badly.

Beddington added that global food reserves are now so low, at a mere 14 per cent of world annual consumption, that a major drought or flood could see food prices rapidly escalate. 'The majority of the food reserve is grain that is in transit between shipping ports,' he said. 'Added to that, the world needs to find 50% more energy and 30% more water.' (3)

There have been warnings over population in the past. In 1968, US environmentalist Paul Ehrlich's book *The Population Bomb* argued that population control measures in the Third World were needed to avert an ecological crisis. Ehrlich predicted that hundreds of millions of people would die of starvation during the 1970s because the population would multiply faster than the world's ability to supply food. Ehrlich's famines never materialised. Like Malthus he was stymied because, although world population grew by more than 50 per cent after 1968, food production grew at an even faster rate due to technological advances.

What could make Malthus relevant again is the fact that agricultural production is totally dependent on fossil fuels, climate and technological advances, in that order. The problem is now too big for us to solve without massive effort. Global population grew by 140 per cent between 1950 and 2000. World population is projected to top nine billion in 2050, up from 6.8 billion this year and 7 billion early in 2012, according to UN estimates. The IPCC has predicted that, whatever happens to greenhouse gases, there will be between 75 and 220 million people in Africa suffering from the effects of severe drought. Around AD 900, the Mayans suffered a prolonged drought that led to the collapse of their civilisation and the abandonment of city-states all across the Yucatan as people migrated in search of a reliable water supply. So where will 200 million Africans go when they run out of water? They will have to go north, to Europe. The latest report on migration by the Organisation for Economic Co-operation and Development (OECD) says African migration to developed countries is marginal in relation to overall flows.

According to the International Organization for Migration, most of the migrants from Africa are now living in Europe. Most travel from North Africa, from Algeria, Morocco and Tunisia. But the Migration Policy Institute believes there are between 7 and 8 million irregular African immigrants living in the EU. That is, those who have entered Europe illegally or without documentation. An increasing number are travelling from Sub-Saharan Africa, from Ghana, Nigeria and Senegal, nearly all of them heading for France, Germany, Italy and the UK.

The prospect of mass migrations concerns Richard Heinberg, the world's foremost authority on peak oil. Heinberg was an adviser on the documentary film *Eleventh Hour,* produced and narrated by film star Leonardo DiCaprio, in 2007. In it, Heinberg says:

> Controlling immigration, which is essential to enabling any nation to control population growth, is enormously controversial, as

immigrants already often face discrimination in many forms. In each case, one or another group would object that human rights were being sacrificed. Yet nature does not negotiate; the Earth is a bounded sphere, and human population growth and consumption growth will be reined in so it appears we must give up at least some human rights if we are to avoid nature's solutions – which have traditionally consisted of famine and disease, as well as the instinctive human response to fight over scare resources... Capital punishment, compulsory infanticide, or abortion – wouldn't adopting these as policy be equivalent to rolling back two or more centuries of gains in humanitarian thinking and social practice? And could such policies ever gain hold in a truly democratic society, or does the avoidance of demographic collapse thus also imply authoritarian governance? I don't think it has to. And I'm not about to give up on humanitarianism. But there is an essential lesson here. If we want peace, democracy, and human rights, we must work to create the ecological condition essential for all these things to exist: i.e. a stable human population at – or less than – the environment's long-term carrying capacity. (4)

If we had the time, the humanist solution would be to encourage the empowerment of women in the Third World. This would bring more jobs, better health services and lower levels of infant mortality, and in developing nations would lead to lower birth rates and the adoption of sustainable growth. The trouble is we haven't got the time, it is already too late. The rate of population increase will win the race to the finish line of world starvation before we have a chance to stop it. Even before the 'perfect storm' of 2030, the developing world will be in a state of severe crisis, its starving peoples migrating north and west.

CHAPTER EIGHT
NEW WORLD DISORDER

Where in the world will be safest for you and your family when global warming starts to play havoc with our climate? Thirty years of freezing temperatures in North America and Western Europe until mid-century followed by a rapid increase in temperatures to the end of the century and beyond will lead to chaos and disorder. The short answer is, inevitably, America.

The UN IPCC panel assumes that the average global temperature will increase by up to 4.5°C (40.1°F) by 2100, and that the sea level will rise by up *No!* to 43cm as a result of water's thermal expansion alone. Moreover, the incipient melting of Greenland's pack ice could significantly alter even that gloomy forecast upwards. The IPCC's February 2007 report concluded that sea-level rises of between 20 and 60cm would occur by 2100. These figures were derived from estimates of how much the sea will increase in volume as it heats up, a process called thermal expansion, and from projected increases in run-off water from melting glaciers in the Himalayas and other mountain ranges. But the report contained very little about the melting ice sheets in Antarctica and Greenland. The IPCC forecast therefore tended to underestimate changes.

According to Dr David Vaughan, of the British Antarctic Survey, 'It is now clear that there are going to be massive flooding disasters around the globe.'

Low-lying areas including Bangladesh, Florida, the Maldives and the Netherlands face catastrophic flooding, while, in Britain, large areas of the Norfolk Broads and the Thames Estuary are likely to disappear by 2100. In addition, British cities including London, Hull and Portsmouth will need radical new flood defences.

This issue dominated the opening sessions of the April 2009 international climate change conference in Copenhagen, a meeting organised to set the agenda for December 2009's international climate talks which aimed to draw up a treaty to replace the current Kyoto Protocol for limiting carbon dioxide emissions.

The trouble is that CO_2 restrictions won't change the atmosphere or the climate. Even if the US now agrees to full compliance with the Kyoto Protocol it will only slightly slow down the growth of CO_2 levels and make almost no impact on global temperature, about 0.02°C by 2050. We must also be aware that CO_2 is not a pollutant or harmful in any way. In fact, it's just the opposite.

Professor David Bellamy, senior lecturer in Botany at Durham University until 1982 and a world-renowned environmental expert, expressed his views on global warming to the national press:

> Carbon dioxide is *not* the dreaded killer greenhouse gas that the 1992 Earth Summit in Rio de Janeiro and the subsequent Kyoto Protocol five years later cracked it up to be. It is, in fact, the most important airborne fertiliser in the world, and without it there would be no green plants at all. That is because, as any schoolchild will tell you, plants take in carbon dioxide and water and, with the help of a little sunshine, convert them into complex carbon compounds – that we either eat, build with or just admire – and oxygen, which just happens to keep the rest of the planet alive. Increase the amount of carbon dioxide in the atmosphere, double it even, and this would produce a rise in plant productivity.

Let me quote from a petition produced by the Oregon Institute of Science and Medicine, which has been signed by over 18,000 scientists who are totally opposed to the Kyoto Protocol, which committed the world's leading industrial nations to cut their production of greenhouse gasses from fossil fuels. They say: 'Predictions of harmful climatic effects due to future increases in minor greenhouse gasses like carbon dioxide are in error and do not conform to experimental knowledge.'

You couldn't get much plainer than that. In other words, climate change is an entirely natural phenomenon, nothing to do with the burning of fossil fuels. In fact, a recent scientific paper, rather un-enticingly titled Atmospheric Carbon Dioxide Concentrations over the Last Glacial Termination, proved it. It showed that increases in temperature are responsible for increases in atmospheric carbon dioxide levels, not the other way around. But this sort of evidence is ignored, either by those who believe the Kyoto Protocol is environmental gospel or by those who know 25 years of hard work went into securing the agreement and simply can't admit that the science it is based on is wrong. The real truth is that the main greenhouse gas – the one that has the most direct effect on land temperature – is water vapour, 99 per cent of which is entirely natural. If all the water vapour was removed from the atmosphere, the temperature would fall by 33 degrees Celsius. But, remove all the carbon dioxide and the temperature might fall by just 0.3 per cent. Although we wouldn't be around, because without it there would be no green plants, no herbivorous farm animals and no food for us to eat.

It has been estimated that the cost of cutting fossil fuel emissions in line with the Kyoto Protocol would be £76 trillion. Little wonder, then, that world leaders are worried. So should we all be. The link between the burning of fossil fuels and global warming is a myth. It is time the world's leaders, their scientific advisers and many environmental pressure groups woke up to the fact. (1)

Here are the winners and losers in the climate stakes lottery that's about to unfold in the next 50 years, with tragic results for millions of people.

UNITED STATES/CANADA

From around 2020, the North American continent will see droughts and high winds that destroy the topsoil in summer reducing the growing season dramatically and freezing winters that play havoc with its infrastructure. America will no longer be the breadbasket of the world. In 2020, it wakes up to the fact it is no longer able to feed its own growing population and announces a moratorium on food exports to other countries.

With only 31 people per square kilometre, America's 305 million inhabitants are well off for natural resources. The food moratorium at last forces Americans to wake up to their wasteful lifestyles. Internal dissent is quelled at the cost of some aspects of America's liberal constitution.

To the south, its borders are besieged by thousands of would-be migrants from Mexico and many other Latin American nations trying to gain entry to the rich resources available in the US after 2020. America becomes a virtual fortress, first by essentially incorporating Canada as its 51st state in a treaty of mutual economic benefit that essentially makes up one economic zone, conditional on America securing its southern borders. Canada's 33 million inhabitants become better off with only three people per sq km now benefiting from the creation of a protectionist block excluding the poorer nations of South America such as Mexico and El Salvador and also further away in Argentina and Chile.

America does this by building a Berlin-type wall across the Mexican border.

The origins of the wall were reported in 2006 by the *Los Angeles Times*. It was the brainchild of Republican F. James Sensenbrenner Jr, who proposed to erect 700 miles of fencing and electric sensors across the Mexican border. The plan for the barrier was approved by the US House in December 2007. In Mexico, the wall became known as el muro. It will use two layers of reinforced fencing, arc lighting, cameras and underground sensors backed up by a heavily armed border militia. One stretch will seal off the entire 350-mile length of the Arizona–Mexico border.

Let's push on to 2025 when the wall is an established fact and has been reinforced with control towers and electronic surveillance linked to robotic-controlled weaponry. The wall is virtually impenetrable but waves of migrants still make suicidal attempts to cross over to the land of plenty. Their desperation is compounded by a lack of fresh water, after agreements that go back to 1944 are torn up by the US government.

The border between Mexico and the USA could well become a major battleground in the near future. Here is a possible scenario for conflict 10 years from now. In 2020, struggling to cope with severe water shortages in Texas, New Mexico and Arizona, the US cuts off the supply of water to Mexico from the Colorado River. US energy supplies are shored up with a hydro-electric power and a water supply treaty with Canada, and reciprocal agreements on the use of nuclear energy. Following the 2008 nuclear power initiative of George W Bush the newly elected Republican administration begins the construction of 25 advanced light water reactor (AWLR) power plants in 2013. These are rushed to completion following Iran's use of a thermonuclear device to obliterate Tel Aviv in 2013 and the subsequent destruction of Teheran by Israeli nuclear weapons. The Middle East descends into anarchy, with oil priced at over $200 a barrel. The US resumes its anti-ballistic missile defence shield based in Europe in 2021 in exchange for massive food aid to the EU, now suffering from a third successive arctic winter and besieged by refugees from Asia and Africa. The refugee problem is particularly severe from the Caribbean islands, where boatloads of starving people, ravaged by successive waves of hurricanes and tornados, are turned back by American warships as they try to gain sanctuary on US soil.

That year, the Posse Comitatus Act of 1878, restricting the military's role in domestic law enforcement, is repealed by Congress at the request of the defence department, whose directive of 2019 warns of great property damage and lives at risk from internal disturbances caused by mass migration and resource wars. America stabilises amid the chaos of world crisis but is beset by chaos raging across the rest of the globe.

ASIA

In China, famine caused by longer winters and hotter summers leaves the country in turmoil. In Bangladesh, storm surges and a higher sea level leave 17 per cent of the country underwater, resulting in 20 million people being made homeless. Many of these people, with nowhere else to go, then begin the long exodus towards Europe.

In 2019, China, Pakistan and India become involved in a border conflict. That year India and Pakistan, now under the control of the Taliban, come close to all-out war after the first use of tactical nuclear weapons in Kashmir province over access to rivers and the use of arable land near their shared borders.

RUSSIA

Russia, with a declining population and huge reserves of natural resources, can weather the short-term freeze and the big heat at the end of the century. It is a nuclear nation and will not want to antagonise its nuclear-armed neighbour to the east, China.

But in the long term one eminent scientist feels that, as the food and water run out in China, around 2030,

Russia's resources will become a prize beyond measurable value, and that conflict will be unavoidable. Russia, because of its low population density, looks to be a winner whichever way the climate goes. The more likely scenario of freezing conditions will see Russia's oil reserves increase astronomically in value. In the longer term, once global warming becomes a fact of life, from 2040 onwards, its frozen tundra will be able to produce copious amounts of surplus food.

Scientist and author John Gribbin sees it this way:

For decades the North American plains have produced a surplus of grain, and one of the biggest consumers of that grain has been the USSR. But the same climate shift that will bring dust-bowl conditions to America will boost agriculture in the Soviet Union. In the main farming region around Moscow yields will go up by almost 50 per cent, provided that steps are taken to introduce varieties that will thrive under the changing conditions. Imagine a world, perhaps only twenty years away, in which the Soviet Union is a major exporter of grain, and the United States has to go cap in hand to be allowed to purchase food to keep its people from going hungry. (2)

Gribbin was referring to a study carried out by the UN Environment Programme in the 1980s (hence the USSR, not Russia) but his point is a valid one. The report also predicted that global warming would benefit cold countries like Finland and Iceland but decimate semi-arid lands like Brazil, Australia, India and Africa. Southern England's climate was predicted to become like that of the south of France, only a lot wetter.

The sheer magnitude of China's population makes war over resources a probability, according to James Lovelock. 'The Chinese have nowhere to go but up into Siberia,' he said. 'How will the Russians feel about that? I fear that war between Russia and China is probably inevitable.' (3)

According to the US Geological Survey, the tundra of north-central Russia has more than 100 billion barrels of recoverable oil beneath its surface. This mighty untapped resource stretches from the Kara Sea to encompass most of Siberia to the west.

The war that begins in the East over access to money-in-the-bank resources like oil and gas will almost certainly be fought over Sakhalin Island, a former penal colony located off the east coast of Russia and to the north of Japan, an island holding vast hydrocarbon resources.

Since the collapse of the former Soviet Union,

Sakhalin has experienced a massive oil boom with petroleum exploration and mining by most oil multinationals. The island's oil and natural gas reserves contain an estimated 14 billion barrels of oil and 80 trillion cubic feet of gas.

Phase 1 of the Sakhalin Island project was focused on oil development and went into production in 1999 at the Vityaz Production Complex. Phase 2 of the project is an integrated oil and gas development that will allow year-round oil and gas production. Of particular importance is the construction of new Liquid Natural Gas (LNG) infrastructure for the convenient export of gas.

After a doubling in the projected cost, the Russian government threatened to halt the project for environmental reasons as a pretext for obtaining a greater share of revenues from the project. Gazprom, Russia's state-owned energy company, took a 50 per cent stake in the project in 2006. That same year, the island's industrial output accounted for 80 per cent of Sakhalin's economy and had become the largest recipient of foreign investment in Russia.

Gazprom is, of course, controlled by the politicians in Moscow. If, in the coming crisis, Putin starts to feel that the price of oil or gas is too low, he may drastically cut production in anticipation of higher prices in the future. On 7 January 2009, Gazprom cut off all gas supplies to Europe travelling through Ukrainian pipelines, a result of the economic crisis that had arisen out of a payments dispute. Fearful European nations, instead of drawing up plans for alternative energy supplies, have instead sought individual contracts with Gazprom, and Russia now supplies a quarter of Europe's gas.

Could this be the wedge that will soon drive Britain away from our special relationship with America and into a new alliance with Russia? It looks unavoidable and the only practical solution given our reliance on imported natural gas. Russia is loaded with dollars and wants to reduce its holdings and come up with an alternative currency to price oil and its other natural resources, especially as the American economy shows signs of going into post-sub-prime meltdown and its currency with it. China is in the same boat.

It will be no surprise if the Russian leadership pushes for this currency to be Russian roubles. If this happens, the dollar will dramatically lose its value as most of the greenbacks now used to buy oil will find their way back to the United States. This means the rate of inflation will rise significantly and commodities such as oil, natural gas, gold, silver and platinum will surge in price.

Russia will be in a position to challenge the dollar by going out and asking for payments in other currencies. When this happens the dollar will be significantly devalued and the price of natural resources will accelerate even more.

In recent years, China's and Russia's relations have become ever more cordial. Chinese President Hu Jintao and Putin met five times in 2007 and laid out the blueprint for development of a strategic partnership. According to the Stockholm International Peace Research Institute, China took delivery of 94 per cent of its conventional weapons from Russia in the five years to 2007. Many analysts fear the beginnings of a new authoritarian bloc, challenging the liberal democratic values of the West.

CHAPTER NINE
LOVELOCK'S DARK AGE

In James Lovelock's view, the scale of the catastrophe that awaits us will soon become obvious. By 2020, droughts and other extreme weather will be commonplace. Miami, Venice and London will be flooded. Food shortages will drive millions of people north, raising political tensions.

Mass migrations will bring epidemics, which will kill millions. By 2100, Lovelock believes the Earth's population will have dipped from today's 6.8 billion to as few as 500 million, with most of the survivors living in the far north, places like Canada, Iceland, Scandinavia, Scotland and the Arctic Basin. By the end of the century, global warming will cause even North America and Europe to heat up by about 14°F. That's double the worst-case scenario predictions of the 2007 report from the IPCC. Recycling, conserving energy and stopping carbon emissions won't make any difference at this late stage, says Lovelock, who believes the sustainable development/carbon trading movement to be a scam to gain profit from disaster.

He told *New Scientist*:

No!

No!

It's wrong to assume we'll survive 2°C (35.6°F) of warming: there are already too many people on Earth. At 4°C (39.2°F) we could not survive with even one-tenth of our current population. The reason is we would not find enough food, unless we synthesised it. Because of this, the cull during this century is going to be huge, up to 90 per cent. The number of people remaining at the end of the century will probably be a billion or less. It has happened before: between the ice ages there were bottlenecks when there were only 2000 people left. It's happening again. (1)

Because of his scientific pedigree, Lovelock simply cannot be discounted as a merchant of doom. In early 1961, he was employed by NASA to develop instruments for the analysis of extraterrestrial atmospheres. Lovelock invented the electron capture detector, which assisted in discoveries about CFCs and their role in ozone depletion. He was elected a Fellow of the Royal Society in 1974 and served as the president of the Marine Biological Association (MBA) from 1986 to 1990.

Lovelock's doomsday scenario makes grim copy; read it and weep.

Rising heat means more ice melting at the poles, which means more open water and land. This is the albedo effect in action where ice reflects sunlight and open land and water absorb it, causing more ice to melt.

Albedo is quantified as the percentage of solar radiation of all wavelengths reflected by a body or surface to the amount that strikes it. A totally white body has an albedo of 100 per cent and a totally black body has zero. So warmer seas expand and rise and increased heat on land leads to precipitation and then intense rainfall in some places, extreme drought in others.

As greenhouse gases begin to build in the atmosphere, temperatures begin to rise and this affects the soil which begins to dry out and the world's forests which begin to die back and burn up. As we have already seen, trees store carbon by photosynthesis. One hectare of tropical rainforest contains up to 250 tonnes of carbon in the form of organic matter, most of which is released by burning. But dead or burned forests (like those being cleared for cattle in the Amazon) turn from being carbon-storage devices to carbon emitters. By 2050, the temperature has risen by more than 8°C over land. Because of increased CO_2 in the atmosphere in the short term (approximately 50 years from now), the Amazon rainforests and the great northern boreal forests, the belt of pine and spruce that covers Alaska, Canada and Siberia will undergo a massive growth spurt. Then they will wither away as this spurt, caused by the increased CO_2 in the atmosphere, leads to shortages of nitrates, phosphorous or potassium in the soil. So growth slows down again, this time permanently. Huge areas of land hidden under the ice are then exposed because of melting ice and this land begins to soak up the sun's rays instead of reflecting them back into space. This permafrost, covering the northern latitudes will thaw, says Lovelock, releasing huge quantities of methane, a greenhouse gas that is 20 times more effective in trapping heat in the atmosphere than CO_2. This methane is presently contained under permafrost which traps lower unfrozen layers of rotting vegetable material still decaying and producing methane. If this permafrost lid melts, the methane in the layers below will escape into the atmosphere. There are also huge quantities of methane gas trapped in ice-like structures in mud and at the bottom of the sea. These ice structures, called clathrates, contain methane in a much more concentrated form than is found in the atmosphere, about 3,000 times more concentrated.

A temperature increase of just a few degrees would cause these ice structures to melt and allow the gas to be released. This would again raise temperatures and release yet more methane. Trapped methane hydrate exists all over the world; there are huge amounts in the Amazon delta and in the Gulf of Mexico. Major rivers carry millions of tonnes of silt containing vegetable matter that continues to decay after the silt is deposited in river deltas. This decay produces methane which gets locked into the silt as methane hydrates until an increase in water temperature is able to release the gas in vast quantities very quickly. Another potentially lethal feedback is the release of this methane from methane hydrates. Methane hydrates actually resemble ice in their physical solidity. What they really are is an unstable mixture of methane and ice formed at very low temperatures and contained by the huge water pressure of the deep oceans. In the Arctic Ocean's colder temperatures, much less pressure is required for these hydrates to form and so when the water there warms up they fizzle up to the surface and disappear into the atmosphere. There could be hundreds of billions of tonnes of these hydrates in the Arctic too far below the ocean's surface to be released at the moment. However, bearing in mind that estimates put the amount of carbon in our atmosphere at 5 billion tonnes, it wouldn't take a great amount of this stored material to be released to cause atmospheric havoc.

This is Lovelock's doomsday scenario of runaway global warming. According to his Gaia hypothesis, in a properly functioning world, these negative feedbacks would be modulated by positive feedbacks, mainly the Earth's ability to radiate heat back into space. But, at a certain tipping point, the regulatory system breaks down and the planet's climate makes a jump to a much hotter state. At the end of the Permian period, 251 million years ago, the release of methane into the atmosphere obliterated almost all life on Earth. This is Lovelock's doomsday.

He says world leaders should now be thinking not of sustainable development but about 'sustainable retreat'. This means it is time to start changing where we live and how we get our food, and making plans for the migration of millions of people from low-lying regions like Bangladesh into Europe. New Orleans is a lost cause, and the money spent on its regeneration after Hurricane Katrina has been wasted. His big idea is that we must preserve our civilisation so that we do not degenerate into barbarism with warlords and gangsters running our affairs and returning us to The Dark Ages.

Lovelock says we now have two choices: we can return to a primitive lifestyle and live at one with the planet as hunter-gatherers, or we can gather up the survivors of the nightmare to come and secure ourselves in a sophisticated, high-tech civilisation.

In the end, it all comes down to where we get our food, water and energy.

For water, the answer is desalination plants, which can turn ocean water into drinking water, but this requires a secure energy supply not based on fossil fuels. Food will be more difficult, as heat and drought will devastate most of today's food-growing regions. People will head north, where they will gather in congested cities with no room to grow anything. Lovelock says the answer is to grow food in huge vats from tissue cultures of meats and vegetables.

He predicts:

What would be synthesised would not be the intricate, natural chemicals we now eat as broccoli, olives, apples, steaks or, more probably, hamburgers and pizzas. Rather, the large new food factories would make simple sugars and amino acids. This would be the feed stock for tissue cultures of meat and vegetables and for junk food made from any convenient organism that could be safely eaten. The technology employed would not be greatly different from that now employed in brewing beer or making antibiotics. By doing this on a scale large enough to feed everyone, the land now farmed could be released back to Gaia and used once again for its proper purpose, the regulation of the climate and chemistry of the Earth. The present over-fishing of the oceans could also cease. (2)

A steady supply of electricity is crucial and Lovelock has no doubt where it must come from. Nuclear power and nuclear fission, in particular, is the only answer. This is because, although supplies of uranium (used as fuel by conventional nuclear power plants) are finite, the energy source used to make nuclear power produced by fast-breeder reactors is virtually limitless.

Unlike, say, gas-cooled nuclear reactors, fission reactors can reprocess plutonium to make more fuel (or nuclear weapons-grade material) and so can actually create more fuel than they consume. The problem is that this type of reactor has proved to be prohibitively expensive in the past. They generate vast amounts of heat but are susceptible to fires and safety-related shutdowns. In France, its fast-breeder Superphoenix reactor managed to stay in operation for less than one year during its first ten years of active life. Lovelock sees fission reactors not as a long-term solution to our energy problems but rather a short-term fix until we can come up with something better. He told one national newspaper, 'We have no time to experiment with visionary energy sources; civilization is in imminent danger and has to use nuclear – the one safe, available energy source – now or suffer the pain soon to be inflicted by our outraged planet.' (3)

It's amazing to think that there were less than 1 billion people alive on Earth in the 1800s; by 1960, that figure had jumped to 3 billion, until today there are roughly 6.8 billion mouths to feed. That figure is expected to rise to 9 billion by 2050.

For Lovelock, this is the essence of the problem. He says:

Population is the whole problem, really. Malthus, a philosopher 200 years ago, was worried about the number of people on the Earth then. In his time there were about a billion, and he said there would be trouble if we went on producing. And he was dead right. If we'd listened to him and stopped then, we wouldn't be in the problem we're in now. With just a billion people, we could do almost anything, and it wouldn't harm the planet – and there would be no further problems. But at six billion and growing the planet just can't cope. We take too much at our current style of living. I'm not just talking about the West, I'm talking about our farming style of living. Once you start herding animals, that's a terribly inefficient way of getting food. You use 20 times as much land as you would if you stayed vegetarian or hunter-gatherer. So, we're all in it – West and underdeveloped world. (4)

When it comes down to just how many people will be alive after the effects of overpopulation coupled with huge energy shortages are taken into account, Lovelock is unequivocal:

When one tries to get at a number, my guess is somewhere between 500 million and 1 billion. No more than that. We will see in this century the most dreadful cull, and people will be driven either to the Arctic basin, which will be the last remaining tolerable climate where food can be grown, or to smaller oases on the continents in the mountainous areas. Ironically, the origins of our species, somewhere in the mountains of Kenya, may be the place where people go back in Africa, and are the last survivors. People fit into the Gaia system in two ways: one, just as another animal, which we are, and we should never forget – we recycle the elements that the plants process and behave just like any other animal – but also because we're intelligent, and we've changed the whole picture of the Earth. (5)

CHAPTER TEN
ANY HOPE? NOT WITHOUT THE AMAZON

On a basic level, we all survive on planet Earth through photosynthesis. Our atmosphere contains billions of tonnes of the gas carbon dioxide, also known as CO_2. Plants breathe in this gas then use the energy of the sun to break the two atoms of oxygen (O2) free from the carbon. The plant then uses this carbon to make carbohydrates and everything else that grows, like roots, leaves, fruit and nuts, most of our food. The plant then breathes out the waste gas, oxygen, that we use to breathe. In this respect, trees and plants are really just air and sunlight in a solid form.

The world's rainforests are both our lungs and our food; without them, we die. Furthermore, when forests are cut down and wood burned, all the carbon stored in the trees by photosynthesis is released into the atmosphere, making it warmer.

The threat to the world's rainforests is of major concern now. These forests that once covered 12 per cent of the world's surface now cover only 5 per cent of it, and that figure is falling. Two-thirds of the world's remaining rainforest is in Brazil, and Brazil is beginning to emerge as a world agricultural superpower. It is now the world's biggest exporter of beef, coffee, orange juice and soy, as well as supplying the burgeoning market for fuel/alcohol product.

Trees and vegetation in the Amazon are estimated to store 90–140 billion tonnes of carbon and have been absorbing CO_2 at a rate of 2 billion tonnes per year in recent decades. The problem is that the Amazon and the rest of the world's forests are being gobbled up by an escalating demand for fuel and food. US-based Rights and Resources Initiative (RRI), an international coalition of forest conservation groups, has warned that, unless steps are taken to hand the people who live on these land masses greater rights, widespread deforestation will make climate change more severe.

Fire clearance, which is actually illegal in the Amazon, releases 400 million tonnes of CO_2 a year into the atmosphere, as much as all the CO_2 released by car emissions in Western Europe in one year. The half life of atmospheric carbon dioxide is about 100 years and it remains in the atmosphere for up to 1,000 years, so even an immediate cessation of all fossil-fuel burning wouldn't make much difference to what's already up there. What scares environmentalists even more is that Brazilian farmers are now chopping down trees at a rate of 25,000 km per year, that's 72 acres every minute, mostly to grow grass to feed cattle. At this rate there will be no Amazon forest left in 50 years.

According to the RRI, the world will need a minimum of 515 million more hectares of land by 2030 in order to grow food, bio-energy and wood products. This is almost twice the amount of land now available and equal to an area 12 times the size of Germany. What happens to all these cattle reared for export? Who consumes it in such vast quantities? Take a close look at your food next time you eat at McDonald's or Burger King. That's where the rainforest is going.

In his acclaimed 1998 study *The Last Hours of Ancient Sunlight*, Thom Hartmann explained:

The most common reason why people are destroying most of the South and Central American rainforests is corporate greed: the American meat habit has provided an economic boom to multinational corporate ranchers, and it is the primary reason behind the destruction of the tropical rainforests of the Americas. Poor farmers and factory farmers alike engage in slash-and-burn agriculture, cutting ancient forests to plant a single crop: grass for cattle. The United States imports two hundred million pounds of beef every year from El Salvador, Guatemala, Nicaragua, Honduras, Costa Rica and Panama, while the average citizen in those countries eats less meat each year than the average American house cat. This deforestation of Latin America for burgers is particularly distressing when you consider that this very fragile area contains 58% of the entire planet's rainforests. (1)

Population pressures mean landless settlers follow the logging companies on to the deforested land and complete the work of destroying the topsoil with intensive agriculture. A recent article in *Nature Geoscience* found that even a 1°C (33.8°F) rise in global temperatures would cause the irreversible loss of huge areas of the Amazon rainforest. Any larger increase would be devastating with 75 per cent of the Amazon rainforest lost for a 3°C (37.4°F) rise and 85 per cent lost for a 4°C (39.2°F) increase.

'A temperature rise of anything over 1°C commits you to future loss of Amazon forest. Even the commonly quoted 2°C target already commits us to

20–40 percent loss,' said the report's lead author Chris Jones. 'On any kind of pragmatic timescale, I think we should see loss of the Amazon forest as irreversible.' (2)

If the Amazon rainforest is lost on this scale, the inescapable conclusion is that this would make warming accelerate because of the massive release of stored CO_2 gas, effectively transforming Earth's largest rainforest from a sink to a source of carbon emissions.

Up until January 1999, the Brazilian government ran a successful rainforest protection project that was used to save and maintain millions of acres of rainforest and the indigenous tribes living there. Under intense pressure from the world's bankers at the IMF, they were forced to slash their budget from $250 million to less than $6 million. Back came armies of loggers, ranchers and farmers, and the destruction began again at a pace.

Studies have shown that trees can offset carbon emissions by absorbing and storing carbon dioxide. The madness of cutting down trees without some efforts at reforestation may turn out to be our gravest error.

James Lovelock would endorse that view. He says:

Our goal should be the immediate cessation of fossil fuel consumption as quickly as possible, and there must be no more natural-habitat destruction anywhere. When I use the term 'natural' I am not thinking only of primeval forests: I include also the forests that have grown back when farmland was abandoned, as happened in New England and other parts of the USA. These re-established forests probably perform their Gaia services as well as did the original forests, but the vast open stretches of monoculture farmland are no substitute for natural ecosystems. We are already farming more than the Earth can afford, and if we attempt to farm the whole Earth to feed people, even with organic farming, it would make us like sailors who burnt the timbers and rigging of their ship to keep warm. The natural ecosystems of the Earth are not just there for us to take as farmland; they are there to sustain the climate and chemistry of the planet. (3)

But, at the eleventh hour, there may be signs that the message is getting through. In June 2008, Brazil launched a large reforestation project to grow 1 billion trees in the Amazon area over a period of five years. The project, One Billion Trees for the Amazon, was launched by President Luiz Inacio Lula da Silva and Ana Julia Carepa, governor of the state of Para, located right in the middle of the rainforest. It will involve 143 municipalities in Para repairing and protecting the Amazon rainforest. This will benefit 120,000 agricultural producers, as well as prevent the emission of over 10 million tonnes of carbon per year. Elsewhere in South America, the Alliance for International Reforestation (AIR), a non-profit organisation, is helping to plant trees, establish tree nurseries and provide environmental education for the people of Guatemala and Nicaragua. Lessons are given showing how to build fuel-efficient brick ovens, dig wells and raise sustainable crops.

The Amazon is Earth's most important carbon sink, keeping carbon locked up in its trees, and the Amazon rainforest needs to become safely ring-fenced from the catastrophic destruction it is now undergoing. This could be paid for by taxing the fast-food chains that are responsible for the rainforest's decline. For these corporate giants, $250 million is a drop in the ocean of corporate profit. They could easily afford to donate 100 times that sum. Or the developed nations could write off Brazil's international debt in return for a commitment to leave the rainforest untouched. If the banking system can be bailed out to the tune of trillions of dollars, surely a fraction of that sum could be used to save the lungs of the planet. Every new acre of rainforest slashed and burned means more carbon gas rather than water vapour being released into the atmosphere. Making the Amazon rainforest a world national park is a matter of urgency.

Chris Turney, a professor of geography at the University of Exeter, has come up with an idea that could stop the long-term effects of CO_2 warming. His research shows that by burying the charcoal produced from microwaved wood the carbon dioxide absorbed by a tree as it grows can remain safely locked away for thousands of years. The technique could take out billions of tonnes of CO_2 from the atmosphere every year. Fast-growing trees such as pine could be produced to act specifically as carbon traps then microwaved, buried and replaced with a fresh crop to do the same thing all over again. Turney says his biochar or biocharcoal technique is the closest thing scientists have to a silver-bullet solution to climate change. Processing facilities could be built right next to forests grown specifically to soak up CO_2. He says, 'You can cut trees down, carbonise them, then plant more trees. The forest could act on an industrial scale to suck carbon out of the atmosphere.'

Turney has built a 5m-long prototype of his microwave, which produces a tonne of CO_2 for $65. He plans to launch his company, Carbonscape, in the UK in order to build the next generation of the machine. This type of charcoal solution has the support of NASA's James Hansen who has calculated that producing biochar could reduce global carbon dioxide levels in the atmosphere by 8ppm over the next 50 years. We could save ourselves through the massive burial of charcoal. It would mean farmers turning all their agricultural waste, which contains carbon that plants have spent the summer soaking up, into non-biodegradable charcoal and burying it in the soil. Large quantities of carbon will be pulled out of the system and reduce CO_2 levels, which should come down quite fast.

In an interview in 2009, James Lovelock was asked whether this technique would make any difference. He replied:

Yes. The biosphere pumps out 550 gigatonnes of carbon yearly; we put in only 30 gigatonnes. Ninety-nine per cent of the carbon that is fixed by plants is released back into the atmosphere within a year or so by consumers like bacteria, nematodes and worms. What we can do is cheat those consumers by getting farmers to burn their crop waste at very low oxygen levels to turn it into charcoal, which the farmer then ploughs into the field. A little CO2 is released but the bulk of it gets converted to carbon. You get a few per cent of biofuel as a by-product of the combustion process, which the farmer can sell. This scheme would need no subsidy: the farmer would make a profit. This is the one thing we can do that will make a difference, but I bet they won't do it. (4)

Our other last best chance appears to be nuclear power, the choice of James Lovelock, who believes the dangers of nuclear power production have been overstated:

The present stock of uranium (used as fuel in power stations) contains only 0.72 per cent of the dangerous isotope U235. From this figure it is easy to calculate that about four aeons (1,000 million years) ago the uranium in the Earth's crust would have been nearly 15 per cent U235. Believe it or not, nuclear reactors have existed since long before man, and a fossil natural nuclear reactor was recently found in Gabon, in Africa... thus life probably began under conditions of radioactivity far more intense than those which trouble the minds of certain present-day environmentalists. (5)

Lovelock is famously pessimistic about our chances of survival beyond this century but he strongly advocates the use of nuclear power, without reservation.

In his preface to Bruno Comby's book, *Environmentalists for Nuclear Energy*, Lovelock states:

Nuclear power, although potentially harmful to people, is a negligible danger to the planet. Natural ecosystems can stand levels of continuous radiation that would be intolerable in a city. The land around the failed Chernobyl power station was evacuated because its high radiation intensity made it unsafe for people, but this radioactive land is now rich in wildlife, much more so than neighbouring populated areas. We call the ash from nuclear power nuclear waste and worry about its safe disposal. I wonder if instead we should use it as an incorruptible guardian of the beautiful places of the Earth. Who would dare cut down a forest in which was the storage place of nuclear ash? Life began nearly four billion years ago under conditions of radioactivity far more intense than those that trouble the minds of certain present-day environmentalists. Moreover, there was neither oxygen nor ozone in the air so that the fierce unfiltered ultra-violet radiation of the sun irradiated the surface of the Earth. We need to keep in mind the thought that these fierce energies flooded the very womb of life. I hope that it is not too late for the world to emulate France and make nuclear power our principal source of energy. There is at present no other safe, practical and economic substitute for the dangerous practice of burning carbon fuels. (6)

Nuclear power on its own will not save us from the coming nightmare; what really needs to change is the obsession that 3 billion people have in the developing world with the American Dream as a model of success. The big-car-driving, all-consuming fossil-fuel-based throwaway economy should never have become the aspiration of economies like India and China. Television advertising played its part in promoting desires that had no historical or cultural precedent. Can we live in a world where a billion Chinese drive an automobile? No, but that is the measure of success common to so many in the developing world and it's too late to change it.

CHAPTER ELEVEN
THE BELL CURVE TOLLS

The change in climate will go in tandem with the end of oil. Not much time remains before easily extracted oil runs out completely, maybe another 30 years. What most geologists are agreed on is that world oil production has already peaked.

Kenneth S. Deffeyes is a geologist who worked with Hubbert in his lab at Shell, and he is equally pessimistic about oil reserves. He says:

> ...published estimates, using variations on Hubbert's methods give peak years from 2004 to 2009. I honestly do not have an opinion as to the peak date for two reasons: 1) the revisions of OPEC reserves may or may not reflect reality; 2) OPEC production capacities are closely guarded secrets... This much is certain: no

initiative put in place starting today can have a substantial effect on the peak production year. No Caspian Sea exploration, no drilling in the South China Sea, no SUV replacements, no renewable energy projects can be brought on at a sufficient rate to avoid a bidding war for the remaining oil. At least, let's hope that the war is waged with cash instead of nuclear weapons. (1)

If the writing is on the wall for Big Oil, the petroleum companies don't seem to be overly concerned. In 1997, BP committed $1 billion to investment in solar-energy research and development and Shell $500 in ? energy renewables. Environmentalists duly noted that, as the global oil industry has a daily turnover of some $2 billion, this paltry sum was nothing other than an attempt by the conglomerates to 'greenwash' public opinion.

Ecologists were not surprised when this report appeared in the national press in December 2007:

Shell, the oil company that recently trumpeted its commitment to a low carbon future by signing a pre-Bali conference communiqué, has quietly sold off most of its solar business. The move, taken with rival BP's decision last week to invest in the world's dirtiest oil production in Canada's tar sands, indicates that Big Oil might be giving up its flirtation with renewables and going back to its roots.

Shell and BP are among the biggest producers of greenhouse gases in the world, but both have been keen to paint themselves green through a series of clean fuel initiatives. BP, under its former chief executive, John Browne, promised to go 'beyond petroleum' while Shell has spent millions advertising its serious interest in the future of the environment. (2)

In 2009, BP cut its investment in alternative energy by almost 30 per cent and Shell has said it will make no significant new investments in wind or solar power in the future. Meanwhile, both are to maintain steady investment in oil and gas exploration.

The *Wall Street Journal* summed up the oil companies' attitude toward renewables in 2009:

As the low oil price reduces cash flow, oil companies find themselves under increasing pressure to invest in their core business and pay high dividends. Investors will demand that every investment dollar generate the maximum return, meaning renewables like wind and solar are likely to get short shrift.

'We are businessmen, and we put the money we have available for investment into the opportunities that give us the best returns for the shareholders,' said Shell's head of gas and power, Linda Cook. 'If those were in renewables today, we'd be putting money there... It's just not the case.' (3)

Since then, BP has been accused by Greenpeace Canada of preparing to commit 'the biggest environmental crime in history'. This follows BP's decision to invest in the extraction of Alberta tar sands, which are said to be five times more energy-intensive to extract compared to traditional oil.

Even as the oil runs out, America will continue its love affair with the motor car, and be joined in an automotive ménage a trois by China and India. If there is one thing that could save the planet from warming in the longer term, it is the gradual abandonment of the use of fossil fuels to power wasteful and inefficient motor cars. President Obama probably knows this but such is the ongoing obsession with the motor car exhibited by the average American family and the financial connections between the large oil corporations and US politicians, it is hard to see how anything can be done. This love affair gathered pace soon after Eisenhower became

President in 1953 and today there are three motor cars for every four American citizens. Backed by the oil corporations, Eisenhower immediately began to push for a system of interstate highways across the United States. Although there were already perfectly adequate federal highways that covered most areas of the country, the interstate highway plan would create 42,000 miles of modern highways. This project became the world's largest public works project and on 29 June 1956 the Federal Aid Highway Act (FAHA) was signed into law and the interstates began to change the face of America.

The FAHA was funded mostly by the taxpayer to the tune of 90 per cent of its cost with the individual states hosting the new roads putting up the other 10 per cent. Almost immediately these new interstate highways became a major stimulus for the chronic suburbanisation and sprawl of cities as, in tandem with the interstates, came smog, traffic congestion and an increasing dependency on the motor car for everything. More importantly, there was a huge decline in subsidy for mass transit, most specifically the railways.

This public subsidy of fossil fuels continues to this day. In 2000, the United States Department of Transportation called for a government-funded injection of $400 billion just to maintain the interstate highway system as it is now. Congress eventually authorised funding for transportation in 2005 of a mind-boggling $286.5 billion, more than the cost of the Marshall Plan that bailed out the whole of Europe after World War II.

Currently, the interstate system is financed by a petrol tax which works out as 18.5 cents on each gallon of petrol bought. Each state sets their own additional petrol tax to help the state pay for their portion of the system. Such is the political influence of the oil conglomerates in America, this tax has not been raised in many years.

If you drive, as you must, along the interstate highways of America, the towns you pass through look depressingly the same, comprising a monotonous ubiquity of Taco Bells, McDonald's, chain stores and petrol stations. These highways killed off the old communities and the small town architecture of Middle America, achingly described in the novels of William Faulkner, Booth Tarkington and Harlan Ellison. They also put paid to the diversity that once flourished in the nation's heartland.

Obama would probably like to privatise the system but he dare not, lest he alienate his conservative gas-guzzling constituents. Americans, while making up only 5 per cent of the world's population, still manage to consume 25 per cent of its energy resources. These are the voters who howled in protest when petrol went up from $1.12 per gallon to $2 in 2000. A system of road tolls could theoretically be used to finance an alternative interstate transport infrastructure in the face of America's trillion dollar deficit, only this time the money would be used to build new railways. Gradually, the goods hauled across country by trucks would be transferred to the subsidised rail network and we would be halfway to solving the global-warming problem Unfortunately, the increased costs of driving will leave many people without transportation.

The good news is that there are moves afoot to do something to encourage increased rail use in America. In 2009, Obama's new government, through the American Recovery and Reinvestment Act, committed to invest an initial $8 billion followed by $1 billion per year for the succeeding five years to develop high-speed rail projects across ten major conurbations.

One of these projects is to be in America's most populous state, California, where the first high-speed train system in the US is to be laid out. Construction of the new high-speed train service will link Southern California, Sacramento, the San Joaquin Valley and the San Francisco Bay Area. Work is set to begin on the new system in 2011 and is scheduled to be completed by 2022 at an estimated cost of $40 billion. The government will provide almost half of the construction costs.

Paying tolls to drive the highways could be one way to stop man-made carbon gases for good, so long as the revenue was used to finance clean energy, but how do you oppose the oil industry when it effectively finances half of the politicians in Congress? Just as the bankers who blew trillions in the credit crunch got back to bonuses as usual once taxpayers had shelled out to save the banks, so will Big Oil join them in their handcart, pursuing profits all the way to the wire, and to hell with the consequences. Many of those with an intimate knowledge of the oil industry and the executives who run it believe that for oilmen the glass will always be half-full, dealing exclusively as they do with issues of wealth creation. In the face of so much evidence on warming and its link to fossil fuels, is it unreasonable to assert that this optimism has coloured the thinking of those who run the business so that their only concern is short-term financial benefits? A philosophy of get in and get out while resources remain on tap, make hay while the sun shines.

Only the intervention of government, it seems, will bring about a change in the fossil-fuel industry, but, even when they do intervene, do they get it right? In 2009, it was reported in the national press that there was 'a boost for green jobs including government funding for a new factory in the north-east, which will make the largest offshore wind blades in the world.

Ed Miliband, Secretary of State for Energy and Climate Change, had given a £4.4m grant to Clipper Windpower to develop offshore wind turbines, with blades 70m long and 175m high, and weighing over 30 tonnes – 'the size of a jumbo jet' – he claimed in a speech to the TUC.

He said:

> With strong government backing, the UK is consolidating its lead in offshore wind energy. We already have more offshore wind energy than any other country, we have the biggest wind farm in the world about to start construction, and now we'll see the biggest turbine blades in the world made here in Britain. Our coastline means the offshore wind industry has the potential to employ tens of thousands of workers by 2020. (4)

The government intends to invest £120 million investment in wind power over the next two years. Part of this will go to Siemens Wind Power which will receive £1.1 million to develop power converters for offshore turbine development.

In the jobs-starved north-east, Clipper, the UK's

only wind-turbine maker, will start work at a new plant next year to develop the blades for its giant turbines. The plant near Blyth, in Northumberland is expected to employ 60 people by the end of 2010. Although a drop in the ocean compared to the energy shortfall expected, the announcement was welcomed by Friends of the Earth as 'exactly the sort of development the government should be supporting'.

Wind power arouses mixed emotions, even within the ecological movement. If wind is to play any part in keeping the lights on after the oil runs out, there has to be massive investment to provide new grid capacity that will allow the transport of wind energy from the remote areas where it is generated to the cities where it will be used.

Some, like Heinberg, are keen on wind power:

How much energy could be derived from the wind? Theoretically, a great deal. A good guide is a 1993 study by the National Renewable Energy Laboratory (NREL) that concluded that about 15 quads [quadrillion BTU] of energy could be produced in the US per year. Since the newer turbines are capable of operating in a wider range of wind conditions, that potential could conceivably now be in the range of 60 quads. Total energy usage in the US is about 100 quads. (5)

James Lovelock is less enamoured of wind power, although he favours its use in strategic locations like the Great Plains of Russia and the US. Lovelock is vehemently opposed to onshore wind farms in Britain (less vehement about offshore wind farms) on the grounds of economics and aesthetics. As he puts it:

To supply the UK's present electricity needs would require 276,000 wind generators, about three per square mile, if national parks, urban, suburban and industrial areas are excluded; also needed would be an efficient way of storing the electricity they produced. But in no way is it efficient and economic; the intermittency of the wind means that, at best, energy is available from wind turbines only 25 per cent of the time. During the remaining 75 per cent, energy has to be made in standby fossil fuel power stations; worse still the power stations have to be kept idling when wind energy is available, an inefficient way for them to operate. The most recent report from Germany put wind energy as being available only 16 per cent of the time. (6)

His point is brought home by the Arctic winter we've just experienced, where a blocking anticyclone deflected our normal wind patterns way to the south for weeks on end. This type of weather pattern is about to become a permanent feature of our winters for 30 years or more.

The best alternative, clean and renewable energy source we have appears to be solar energy, and here Japan leads the world. Faced with low energy reserves, a dense population structure and limited fossil-fuel reserves, Japan began investing heavily in solar power in the early 1990s.

In one hour, the sun beams down enough clean renewable energy to supply all the Earth's energy requirements. Up until recently, capturing all that energy in a low Energy Return on Energy Invested (EROEI) ratio has been a major difficulty. That is the amount of usable energy you can take from any specified energy resource, like wind or oil, set against the amount of energy used to obtain it. It's no use having a photovoltaic (PV) cell which gives out £9 worth of energy if it cost £10 to make. Silicon-based solar cells account for 92 per cent of our current PV market, but they are very expensive to manufacture. However, with Japanese technology to the rescue, their cost will soon be reduced by a tenth with the introduction of super-thin PVs made with much cheaper materials. The most promising of these new materials is buckyballs, a conductive polymer covered with nano-size molecules (the buckyballs). Japanese electronic giant Matsushita Electric Industrial has developed these solar coatings that could theoretically be painted on clothes, tents, roofs and walls. The heat generated could then be used to power just about anything. Germany is fast catching up with Japan's solar lead. Its Siemens Solar Group has applied a thin coating of the buckyball mixture on to thin plastic making the cost of these solar panels even less. Researchers believe that efficiency can be increased by up to 100 per cent so that a solar coating applied to a household roof could supply all the electricity needed.

In January 2009, the Japanese government declared its goal of increasing solar-power generation by 40 times its current level by 2030 with an investment of $56 billion to create the necessary infrastructure development. Japanese Prime Minister Taro Aso says he wants solar-power generators installed in 37,000 Japanese schools over the next three years and beyond 2012 is confident that solar power and electric cars will lift Japan out of a seemingly intractable recession.

Whatever type of substitute renewable is put in place, the people of Britain are about to face the biggest challenge to their survival as a nation state since we stood alone against Hitler in 1940. It is now too late to emerge from this challenge unscathed, but if policymakers act now we could emerge battered but still standing by the time the Arctic weather retreats.

That period will see the last cheap fossil fuels being exhausted, so we need to start investing now in a mix of renewables – nuclear power as a short-term solution, as well as offshore wind farms and tidal-wave generation. There must also be investment in combined heat and carbon capture power stations. All immigration must cease immediately, only those with outstanding technical skills would be exempt. The tax and benefit system should be restructured to penalise anyone having more than one child and those illegal immigrants still in Britain, estimated at more than 500,000, must be removed. To make these necessary changes, we will need to leave the EU, unless there is general agreement that we can implement our sovereign policy without interference. This would also allow us to change our methods of farming from the current predominantly industrial agricultural set-up, dictated by the EEC and unsuitable for such a small nation as ours, to a greater reliance on smaller farms within the context of rural communities. On these farms, our army of unemployed can be taught agronomy and learn how to produce enough food to set us on the road to greater self-sufficiency (given a smaller population over time).

The world urgently needs to get ready for the end of the fossil-fuel era and be willing to make big sacrifices to prevent a crisis. We don't have much time. We could go on as we are for another ten years and nothing much would change, except for the weather, but come the next decade it will be too late. What needs to happen now is the immediate agreement of governments from all around the world to save what is left of the fossil-fuel base and use it to finance and then put into place sustainable energy sources. That means phasing out the use of petrol-driven motor vehicles straight away, building no more airport runways and subsidising mass public transport in our towns and cities. The clock is running down, ten years at the outside, but we need to get moving.

CHAPTER TWELVE
YOUR LIMITED CHOICE

The UN climate conference in Copenhagen did not produce a deal on climate change. Instead, the leaders of 193 nations ended up signing a non-binding pact that made vague promises to fight global warming. The final agreement reached was not a treaty and had no internal or external enforcement mechanisms.

They also failed to reach an agreement on new targets for reducing greenhouse-gas emissions and the provision of financial aid to poor countries in their efforts to limit climate change.

The main dispute was between the world's biggest polluters, the US and China. On reflection, it appears that China and India were in no mood to sign anything that could imperil their emergence as industrial giants. Between them, they managed to stifle any meaningful or productive discussion between the major emitters. A commitment to prevent global temperatures breaching a 2°C (35.62°F) threshold by 2020 was removed and replaced by vague suggestions that emissions should peak 'as soon as possible'. The long-term target of global emission cuts of 50 per cent by 2050 never even got out of the starting gate.

No!

Predictably, President Obama was roasted by the ecologists and aid agencies in print, but that may not have been the real story. China's spectacular industrial growth this century and its global political and economic dominance is based largely on cheap coal. China knows it is now a superpower and it has its coal-based industry to thank for it. With national wealth doubling every decade, it's possible China's leaders did not want to kill off their golden goose by making a deal that limited carbon emissions.

Obama went to Copenhagen with the hope of getting a deal, which he needed to show a hostile Senate at home that he could bring China to heel on climate. His conservative opponents have long argued that US carbon cuts would further boost a booming China to the detriment of the US economy. Their agenda has always been to raise the indignation of the American public by demanding that any emission cuts made by America be linked to polluting countries like

India and China: if the US makes cuts, then so should they. For the Chinese, the counter-argument goes that the US, with only 5 per cent of the world's population, manages to emit 20 per cent of all greenhouse gases.

Maybe this is why the average American didn't bother to recycle, generating twice the amount of rubbish as the average citizen of Germany or Italy. The US economy has gradually become dependent on artificial patterns of living subsidised by cheap fossil fuel. They rely on cars to get everywhere, computers to do the work, and electricity to cook and to entertain. Everywhere is conspicuous consumption and waste, and the result is a nation ill on plenty with 64 per cent of its adult population officially obese. Is it any wonder that starving nations in the Third World, observing this cornucopia of waste beamed to them on satellite TV, should protest that as the developed world's wealth has been accumulated from past use of fossil fuels why should they be denied the chance to catch up using the same resource? Surely any climate negotiations should reflect the rich West's indebtedness to the environment for their favoured position and that it would be more just to have much stricter emissions targets for the developed world in tandem with a massive transfer of clean technology to poor countries, bought and paid for by the US in particular, as the Earth belongs to us all, in general.

China isn't going to be left out of the rich nations club just as it's getting its foot in the door, but China is concerned enough about the dire consequences of global warming to be investing heavily in both wind and solar power.

Is the failure to reach agreement at Copenhagen necessarily the catastrophe it has been portrayed as? For ecologists, the hoped-for outcome was carbon-cap measures that would have restricted wealth-producing industry worldwide. It did not achieve the reduction required to slow the predicted warming, but, if the failure of Copenhagen is a temporary stall on the way to a longer-term resolution committing the US and China to binding and verifiable agreements, this is better than a treaty which does nothing other than paper over the cracks by allowing continued globalisation and taking no action on fossil fuels and population.

Another problem was that decisions were going to be made without a clear scientific consensus on how much of global warming is due to the actions of the sun.

Eminent astrophysicist John Gribbon thinks we need to broaden our historical perspectives:

The world has rarely been as cold as it is today. We don't call it an Ice Age, because not too long ago the world was even colder than it is today –

that is what we think of as 'the' Ice Age. Before too long, unless human activities prevent it, the world will be cool again, back to the Ice Age proper. Our perspective (the entire history of human civilisation) embraces only a short-lived, temporary retreat of the ice, an interglacial. (1)

If a supercomputer at Hadley Centre cannot predict the weather accurately more than a week in advance, is it possible that we are being overly pessimistic about the current warming phase. It is entirely possible that man-made global warming is a short-lived phenomena and that the detrimental effects of higher concentrations of carbon dioxide in our atmosphere will be absorbed without a crisis and we will once again return to the usual pattern of glacial and interglacial periods. We still don't know.

The need to answer these questions quickly is a matter of life and death, because for Britain, Western Europe and parts of North America our immediate worry is not long-term warming but short-term cooling.

The latest observations taken from space in April 2009 show that the sun is the dimmest it has been for nearly a century and these results are worrying astronomers who will study these new pictures at the next UK National Astronomy Meeting. They show an almost unprecedented absence of sunspots and solar flares, with the sun having entered into a period of almost complete inactivity. The strength of the solar wind is at a 50-year low, radio emissions are at a 55-year low, and sunspot activity is at a 100-year low.

As we have seen, the sun normally undergoes an 11-year cycle of activity. At its peak, it spits out flares and planet-sized chunks of super-hot gas, followed by a calmer period. Last year, it was expected to get hotter but instead it hit a 100-year low. The usual 11-year cycle of activity isn't repeating as normal.

Measurements by NASA's Ulysses spacecraft in 2009 revealed a 20 per cent drop in solar wind pressure since the mid-1990s – the lowest point since such measurements began in the 1960s. Measurements by several other NASA spacecraft have also shown that the sun's brightness has dimmed by 0.02 per cent at visible wavelengths and a massive 6 per cent at extreme UV wavelengths since the solar minimum of 1996.

In the mid-17th Century, the Maunder minimum period lasted 70 years, and led to a mini ice age. Research papers ready for publication will suggest we may well be heading for another Maunder minimum period. Scientists cannot say precisely how big the coming cooling will be, but it could be enough to offset the current impact of man-made global warming, albeit temporarily.

Sami Solanki, of the Max Planck Institute for Solar System Research, says declining solar activity could reduce global temperatures by 0.2°C. In January 2007, the Russian Academy of Sciences' astronomical observatory reported that global cooling would develop within 50 years. Khabibullo Abdusamatov, head of the agency's space research branch, saw the coming period of global cooling as similar to one seen in the late 17th century. It will start in 2012–2015 and reach its peak in 2055–2066. 'The global temperature maximum has been reached on Earth, and Earth's global temperature will decline to a climatic minimum even without the Kyoto Protocol,' he said.

There is recent research suggesting that solar variability can have a very strong regional climatic influence on Earth – in fact, stronger than any man-made greenhouse effect and that could force a revision of what we believe to be true about man-made warming. We may have overestimated the sensitivity of the Earth's atmosphere to an increase of carbon dioxide from the pre-industrial three parts per 10,000 by volume to today's four parts per 10,000. This may give Britain some breathing space in the face of rising temperatures over the next 50 years, but we cannot be complacent. We can push back the day of reckoning but eventually we will have to deal with the consequences of a warmer

Earth. For Britain and Western Europe, this is the most likely scenario.

We have already begun to experience colder winters and shorter wetter summers. This will accelerate to reach a peak around 2025 when most of Britain will be ice-bound between December and April every year until approximately 2040 when the effects of global warming outside of Europe will first thaw us out and then heat us up in line with the rest of the world.

From 2013, Britain will become progressively battered by severe storms coming from the Atlantic. Freezing winters will reduce our output and there will be severe shortages of both food and fresh water from 2025 onwards.

While we shiver, in Australia, South America and southern Africa, the heat starts to become unbearable. Drought persists in these areas, where average rainfall has declined by more than 25 per cent by 2025. Asia is also hard hit by storms and drought. There is a strong possibility of war in the East, including the use of nuclear weapons by 2030.

America becomes a fortress nation and effectively seals its borders after 2025, Europe is besieged by refugees and its infrastructure begins to crumble by 2030.

New authoritarian regimes spring up in place of liberal democracies throughout the former EU states, as the price of food, energy and water begins to increase exponentially. Those with advance warning have put their money into stock options related to these basic utilities. Others invest in gold as the currency markets begin to fluctuate wildly and the American economy, burdened by debt, ceases to be the world's reserve currency. The dollar is abandoned as the unit of global trade and the world is bounced into economic protectionism. However, even this foresight will not save those who thought they had made wise financial investments. As soon as it becomes evident that the era of continuous economic growth, based on the consumption of fossil fuels is over, the market crashes permanently. The casino economies that have relied on false confidence and false assurances from the OPEC nations are finished. The individuals who hedged their bets and hoarded their gold find that even those riches are unable to buy them the necessities of life.

By 2030, millions are dying across the globe. Those who can afford the prohibitive visa entry fee will try to take themselves and their families to the relatively safe haven of US/Canada. The rest will die in their billions as by 2050 the Four Horsemen of the Apocalypse, pestilence, famine, war and death, are rampaging across the globe unchecked.

This is what lies in store for all of us, a period of

turmoil and fear as the world adjusts to its future without the cushion of fossil fuel. The proof of it is that behind the scenes US strategic planners are already considering what action to take to preserve our knowledge and civilisation for future generations should the worse come to the worst. Plans that would once have been dismissed as belonging to the realms of science fiction are now being undertaken.

In 2006, NASA announced plans to construct a solar-powered outpost at one of the moon's poles, with the lunar base to be permanently staffed by 2024, while in Europe preparations for a possible environmental doomsday are well advanced. In February 2006, the Norwegian government unveiled plans for the Svalbard Global Seed Vault, a fortress that will contain up to 3 million seed varieties on a remote island 600 miles from the North Pole.

The project is the first comprehensive effort to protect the world's agricultural gene pool. The Svalbard facility will be a backup to the fragmentary and loosely organised collections around the world safeguarding roughly 1.5 million varieties of plant against crop failure. It will preserve the DNA of every crop on the planet along with wild relatives. The vault was completed in 2007 at a cost of roughly $6 million.

There are other proposals from NASA to place the first experimental genetic databank on the moon by

2020, and having the full database in place by 2035, roughly 20 years before the most devastating effects of global warming are predicted to cause serious disruptions in human food supply and mass extinction.

The databank would need to be buried under rock to protect it from the extreme temperatures, radiation and vacuum on the moon. It would be run partly on a mix of solar power and nuclear fission and the information stored would be a repository for the DNA of every single species of plant and animal life on Earth as well as a record of human history, technological progression and cultural milestones. These would be recorded in Arabic, Chinese, English, French, Russian and Spanish, and would be linked by transmitter to 4,000 'Earth repositories' that would provide shelter, food and a water supply for survivors of the environmental catastrophe planners believe is on its way by 2030.

Those allowed to gain entry to these repositories would be restricted to a well-educated political, scientific and economic elite carefully selected as the standard bearers of a new world order.

This lunar ark, maintained by robotic technology, would also play host to a few chosen humans. As Professor Dr Bernard H. Foing, Chief Scientist of ESA's Research and Scientific Support Department explained:

To develop a true Noah's Ark, we eventually would need to bring people to the moon. Only humans could do all the things necessary to successfully operate a genetic laboratory. On Earth we are already investigating several activities such as genetic sequencing, cloning, and stem cell research. Our lunar scientists could adapt that technology – cultivating cells, storing them, and doing experiments to ensure that embryology works on the moon. (2)

How many will be left to bear witness to this irony? The final repository of a failed civilisation, sending messages to a ravaged planet a quarter of a million miles away.

GLOSSARY

8,000-Year Event – a sudden drop in temperature in the North Atlantic Ocean approximately 8,000 years ago.

acre-foot – 271, 328 gallons of water.

AIR – Alliance for International Reforestation

albedo effect – the amount of sunlight reflected from a surface.

ALWR – advanced light water reactor

AO – Arctic Oscillation

Big Oil – Collective term for oil and gas conglomerates.

BTU – British Thermal Unit; 1 BTU is equal to 1.06 Kilojoules of energy, the amount of energy needed to heat one pound of water to 1°F

buckyballs – a molecule of carbon able to conduct heat.

carrying capacity – the number of people who can be supported within given limits of natural resources.

clathrates – a compound in which methane is trapped.

CLIWOC – Climatological Database for the World's Oceans

denier – someone who denies Global Warming is a fact.

EIA – Energy Information Agency

EROEI – Energy Return on Energy Invested

EU – European Union

FAHA – Federal Aid Highway Act

FAO – UN Food and Agriculture Organization

GISP2 – Greenland Ice Sheet Project II

Great Ocean Conveyor – ocean circulation system driven by density gradients.

GRIP – Greenland Ice Core Project.

Holocene period – The Age of Man, this period of 10,000 years since the last ice age.

IMF – International Monetary Fund

interglacial – a geological interval of warmer temperature separating ice ages.

IPCC – Intergovernmental Panel on Climate Change

Kyoto Protocol – an international agreement setting targets for the reduction of greenhouse gas emissions.

Little Ice Age – An interval of cold temperature within an interglacial.

LNG – Liquid Natural Gas

Maunder minimum – The period of solar inactivity between 1645 and 1710.

MBA – Marine Biological Association

MDOs – multi-decadal oscillations

Met Office Hadley Centre – UK climate change research centre.

MOC – Meridional Overturning Circulation

MVP – Medieval Warm Period

NAO – North Atlantic Oscillation

NERC – Natural Environment Research Council

NREL – National Renewable Energy Laboratory

OECD – Organisation for Economic Co-operation and Development

OPT – Optimum Population Trust

ppm – parts per million

PV –photovoltaic

quadrillion – equal to the amount of energy available from 45 million tonnes of coal or 170 million barrels of crude oil

RRI – Rights and Resources Initiative

Schwab cycle – an 11-year cycle of maximum to minimum sunspot activity.

solar cycle 24 – the next solar cycle , set to peak in 2013.

Spörer minimum – 90 years of solar inactivity between 1460 and 1550.

sunspots – dark spots of reduced surface temperature caused by intense magnetic activity

THC – thermohaline circulation

thermal expansion – change in volume of water in response to a change in temperature.

UN – United Nations

WHOI – Woods Hole Oceanographic Institution

Younger Dryas – A return to freezing conditions 12,700 years ago.

BIBLIOGRAPHY

Introduction
(1) *Daily Mail*, David Rose, 10/1/2010
(2) Telegraph.co.uk, 1/1/2010

Chapter 2
(1) R.B Alley, *The Two-Mile Time Machine* (2000).
(2) M.K. Hughes and H.F. Diaz, Was there a Medieval Warm Period? *Climatic Change*, v26, p109–142 (1994).
(3) Cook, Palmer and D'Arrigo, Evidence for a Medieval Warm Period in a 1,100 Year Tree-ring Reconstruction of Past Austral Summer Temperatures in New Zealand. *Geophysical research letters*, vol 29, No 14 (2002).
(4) Robert B. Gagosian, lecture at the World Economic Forum Davos, Switzerland. Climate change: Should we be worried? 27 January 2003.
(5) Harry L Bryden et al, Slowing of the Atlantic

meridional overturning circulation at 25°N. *Nature*, 438, 1 December 2005.

(6) W.S. Broecker, Climatic change; are we on the brink of a pronounced global warming? *Science*, v189, n 4201, p460–463 (1975).

(7) H.L. Bryden text to G.M. Cooke, 14 February 2009.

(8) Fred Pearce, Berks at NERC snub Peter Wadhams, again. *Daily Telegraph*, 10 November 2008.

(9) James Lovelock, *The Revenge of Gaia* (2006) p55.

Chapter 3

(1) Richard Heinberg, *The Party's Over: Oil War and the Fate of Industrial Societies* (2003) p124.

(2) Richard Heinberg, op cit (2003) p196.

(3) *Sunday Times*, 4/1/2009.

(4) Jonathan Porritt, ed., *Planet Earth, the Future* (2006) p108.

Chapter 4

(1) IPCC report, 2001.

(2) Technology Review, 2004.

(3) House of Lords Select Committee on Economic Affairs produced a report on the economics of climate change, 2005.

(4) Hays, Imbrie and Shackleton paper in *Science* in 1976, Variations in the Earth's Orbit: Pacemaker of the Ice Ages.

(5) Henrik Svensmark, Proceedings of the Royal Society Journal A: Mathematical, Physical and Engineering Sciences, 2006.

(6) Climatic Warming in North America: Analysis of Borehole Temperatures. *Science*, v268, p1576–1577, 16 June 1995.

(7) BBC News, 21 May 2009.

(8) G.M. Cooke, interview with Dr D. Wheeler, Sunderland University, 12 March 2009.

Chapter 5

(1) E. Friis-Christensen and K. Lassen, Length of the Solar Cycle: An indicator of solar activity closely associated with climate. *Science*, v254, p698–700, 1991.

(2) David Adam, *Guardian*, 19 August, 2005.

(3) From October 2000 Proceedings of the National Academy of Sciences (USA).

(4) Solar Cycle 24: Implications for the United States to the International Conference on Climate Change.

(5) Science@Nasa by Dr Tony Phillips.

(6) Sami K. Solanki, Ilya G. Usoskin, Bernd Kromer, Manfred Schüssler, Jürg Beer, Unusual activity of the sun during recent decades compared to the previous 11,000 years. *Nature*, 28 October 2004

(7) Sami K. Solanki and Natalie A. Krivova, Can solar variability explain solar warming since 1970? *Journal of Geophysical Research*, 108, 2003.

(8) Ilya G. Usoskin, Sami K. Solanki, Manfred Schüssler, Kalevi Mursula and Katja Alanko. *A Millennium Scale sunspot Reconstruction: Evidence for an Unusually Active Sun since the 1940s.*

(9) H. Svensmark and G. Calder. *The Chilling Stars: A New Theory of Climate Change.*

(10) *Science*, 11 February 2000.

(11) In a lecture on 18 April 2008 at the RAS-sponsored National Astronomy meeting in Preston.

(12) *Sun, Earth, Man: A Mesh of Cosmic Oscillations – How Planets Regulate Solar Eruptions, Geomagnetic Storms, Conditions of Life and Economic Cycles; Urania Trust* (Mar 1989), ISBN-10: 1871989000.

(13) T. Landscheidt (2000b). River Po discharges and cycles of solar activity. *Hydrol. Sci. J.* 45:491–493.

(14) Landscheidt, T. (2000d). New confirmation of strong solar forcing of climate.

(15) Landscheidt, T. (2000e). Solar wind near Earth: Indicator of variations in global temperature. *ESA-SP* 463,497-500.

Chapter 6

(1) Report by Peter Schwartz and Doug Randall commissioned by the Pentagon and published on 1 October 2003.

Chapter 7

(1) *Rolling Stone*, October 2007.
(2) L.R. Brown and B. Halweil, Worldwatch Institute, www.worldwatch.org. Unfpa state of world population 2001: footprints and milestones – population and environmental change, www.unfa.org
(3) Prof. Beddington, interview with Ian Sample, *Guardian*, 18 March 2009.
(4) Richard Heinberg, *Peak Everything* (2007) p121.

Chapter 8

(1) Global Warming? What a load of poppycock! *Daily Mail*, 9 July 2004.
(2) John Gribbin, *Hothouse Earth, the Greenhouse Effect and Gaia* (1990) p220.
(3) James Lovelock, *Rolling Stone*, 1/11/2007

Chapter 9

(1) James Lovelock, *New Scientist*, 23/1/2009.
(2) James Lovelock, *The Revenge of Gaia* (2006) p133.
(3) *Independent*, 24 May 2004.
(4) Jonathan Porritt, op cit (2006) p104.
(5) Jonathan Porritt, op cit (2006) p119.

Chapter 10

(1) *The Last Hours of Ancient Sunlight* (1998) p50.

(2) Chris Jones, Copenhagen Climate Conference, March 2009.

(3) James Lovelock, op cit (2006) p12.

(4) One last chance to save mankind, interview by Gaia Vince. *New Scientist*, 23 January 2009.

(5) James Lovelock, *Gaia, A New Look at Life on Earth* (1979) p15.

(6) James Lovelock, Preface, *Environmentalists for Nuclear Energy*, by Bruno Comby.

Chapter 11

(1) Kenneth S Deffeyes, *Hubbert's Peak*, p149.

(2) Terry MacAlister, *Guardian*, 11/12/2007.

(3) James Heron, *Wall Street Journal*, 25/3/2009.

(4) Helene Mulholland, *Guardian*, 12/9/2009.

(5) Richard Heinberg, op cit (2003) p154.

(6) James Lovelock, op cit (2006) p83.

Chapter 12

(1) John and Mary Gribbin, *Ice Age* (1990) p1.

(2) *Astrobiology Magazine*, 27 February 2006.

FURTHER READING

James E. Lovelock. *The Revenge of Gaia: Why the Earth is Fighting Back - and How We Can Still Save Humanity* published by Allen Lane, 2006.

Tim Jackson. *Prosperity without Growth – Economics for a Finite Planet* Earthscan, 2009.

James Hansen. *Storms of my Grandchildren.* Bloomsbury, 2009.

John D. Cox. *Climate Crash: Abrupt Climate Change and What it Means for Our Future.* Joseph Henry Press, 2005.

Andrew E. Dessler and Edward A. Parson. *The Science and Politics of Global Climate Change: A Guide to the Debate.* Cambridge University Press, 2006

Tim Flannery. *The Weather Makers: How Man is Changing the Climate and What it Means for Life on Earth.* Atlantic Monthly Press, 2006.

Al Gore. *An Inconvenient Truth.* Rodale Press, 2006.

Henry N. Pollack. *Uncertain Science ... Uncertain World*. Cambridge University Press, 2003

Sebastian Junger. *The Perfect Storm.*W. W. Norton, 1997.

William D. Nordhaus and Joseph Boyer. *Warming the World: Economic Models of Global Warming.*MIT Press, 2000.

National Research Council and Ocean Studies. *Abrupt Climate Change: Inevitable Surprises.*National Academy Press, 2002.

Lester Brown. *Who Will Feed China? Wake-up Call For a Small Planet*. WW Norton, 1995.

Kenneth S. Deffeyes. *Hubbert's Peak: The Impending World Oil Shortage*, Princeton University Press, 2001.

Thom Hartmann. *The Last Hours of Ancient Sunlight: Waking Up to Personal and Global Transformation*. Mythical Books, 1998.

Chris Turney. *Ice, Mud and Blood*. Macmillan,2008

John Gribbin. *Hothouse Earth: The Greenhouse Effect & Gaia*. Bantam Press, 1979.

James Lovelock. *Gaia:A New Look at Life on Earth*. Oxford University Press, 1979.

John Imbrie and Katherine Palmer Imbrie. *Ice Ages: Solving the Mystery*. Macmillan Press, 1979.

Richard Heinberg. *The Party's Over: Oil , War and the Fate of Industrial Societies*. Clairview 2003.

Richard Heinberg. *Peak Everything*. Clairview 2006.